Parents
On Your Side ®

by Lee Canter
and Marlene Canter

A Publication of Canter & Associates, Inc.

Project Leader
Marcia Shank

Editorial Staff
Carol Provisor
Pat Sarka
Kathy Winberry

Contributing Editor
Bob Winberry

Design
The Arcane Corporation

© 1991 Canter & Associates, Inc.
P.O. Box 2113, Santa Monica, CA 90407-2113
800-262-4347   310-395-3221
www.canter.net

Printed in the United States of America
First Printing January 1991

04 03 02 01 00   15 14 13 12 11

Library of Congress Catalog Card Number 91-6598
ISBN #0-939007-39-8

PD4006

This book is
dedicated to the memory of
Paul Bell, former superintendent of Dade
County Schools. His love for children,
parents and teachers will always
serve as an inspiration to us.
Paul, we will all miss you.

Acknowledgments

We would like to give our heartfelt thanks to the following friends and associates whose contributions to *Parents On Your Side* are deeply appreciated.

Ellen Doukoullos

Dr. George Ethridge

Linda Manuel

Lil Mikelman

Carol Provisor

Pat Sarka

Barbara Schadlow

Sandi Searls

Marcia Shank

Jim Thompson

Kathy Winberry

Contents

Introduction

Several years ago in Indianapolis I sat with a group of educators, listening to them speak of the frustration they were experiencing in their jobs. The feelings each of them expressed bore a striking similarity:

"I feel alone in my classroom. This isn't like it should be."

"There should be a team effort, but there isn't."

"My students come to school overtired and unfed. How am I supposed to teach them?"

"I'd like parent involvement, but I don't know how to begin to work with parents."

"I can go only so far in the classroom on my own. I need parents to support me."

The frustration these teachers felt was certain. So too was their shared professional goal and main concern: *We want our students to succeed.*

As I listened, I was struck by the paradox of what they were saying.

These teachers needed parent support to do their jobs successfully, yet they did not have that support and in some cases weren't sure if they wanted it or—if they wanted it—how to get it. As a result, these teachers were missing a vital ingredient necessary for their students to achieve their highest potential. They were missing the active support of parents.

Schools can't do it alone. You can't do it alone.

The education of children is a responsibility that must be shared by you the teacher and parents alike. We need to recognize what a powerful asset a parent can be; what a powerful component parents are to a child's success. To work effectively, you need parents to support your academic, disciplinary and homework efforts.

Experience has no doubt shown you that you will encounter many types of parents during your teaching career: parents who gladly give the support you need; parents who want to help, but don't know how; parents who are angry at schools in general; parents who seem to be incapable of handling their own lives, let alone the lives of their children; and, finally, parents who really just don't care.

Reaching all of these parents, and gaining their support, may seem to be a tough assignment at best. But you can do it. Our goal in writing *Parents On Your Side* is to empower you to be a more successful teacher by showing you how to get the support you need from parents—all kinds of parents.

Every parent, in his or her own way, can support you. The value you place on each child's education, and the manner in which you communicate that attitude to parents, can transcend varying family circumstances, ethnic and cultural diversity, poverty and apathy. You *can* expect and receive cooperation. By establishing positive relationships with parents, and by conscientiously maintaining these relationships throughout the year, you will find that even the most difficult or apathetic parents can be motivated to give support.

What could you anticipate if you could get all the parents to support your academic, discipline and homework efforts? Take a look at the students you deal with today. Think of the difficulties you are having motivating some of these students to reach their full potential. Now imagine for a moment that you had all the parents of your students backing you 100%. Imagine that you could pick up the phone and get parents to give you the cooperation you need when their child is not doing his or her work, not behaving in class, or not completing homework assignments. Think of the results you would achieve with your students. The results would be dramatic. If and when you had all the parents backing your efforts, your ability to help your students succeed would increase profoundly.

Marlene and I hope that *Parents On Your Side* will help you reach this goal, and in doing so help your students achieve their highest potential.

Parents
On Your Side

Chapter 1

Why You Need Parents On Your Side

66 *Stephanie just doesn't seem to care about school. She rarely does her homework and most of the time she isn't prepared for class. She could be an A student, but she is barely doing C work. I've spoken to her parents. They said they would make sure she starts doing her homework, but they don't follow through.* 99

"Chris was a problem in class all day today—constantly talking back, yelling and screaming. I tried reaching his mother. She's never at home and she's told me not to call her at work. She doesn't want to be bothered. She said that there's nothing she can do with her son."

"Nothing I've tried has worked with Michael. He just sits there and won't work. Do you know what his mom said when I called her? She said that during the day he was my responsibility. She said that I am the teacher and I should be able to get him to do his work."

Sound familiar? If so, you're not alone. Educators today are called upon to teach more and more students with academic and behavior problems, as well as students who are just not motivated to do their best in school. Complicating this situation is the reality that all too often these students have parents who seem unwilling or unable to become involved in their children's education.

Lack of parental support from the parents of Stephanie, Chris and Michael resulted in their teachers having to handle these situations on their own—with less than positive results. These teachers' frustration mirrors the frustration of many educators today who attempt to motivate students without the active support of parents.

How important is parent support? Think about this: Why did you behave in school? Why did you strive to succeed academically? If you were like many others, your parents were an important factor in shaping your attitude toward school.

"In our home we had two rules about school. Rule #1 was: Do what the teacher says; do your best work; never misbehave. Rule #2 stated that under no circumstances were we ever to break Rule #1. My parents always let us know that they were prepared to do whatever it took to ensure that we succeeded in school. And I knew that they meant it.

"Looking back now, I can see that my parents really empowered my teachers. When my teacher stood in front of the class, my parents were standing symbolically at his or her side. A request from my teacher was a

request from my parents. A demand from my teacher was a demand from my parents. If I got into trouble at school, I got into twice as much trouble at home. My parents never felt that either my teacher or the school were responsible for me. My parents always knew that they themselves were key to my success. They knew that their interest, involvement and expectations provided the motivation I had to have to achieve my potential.

"Today I'm a teacher, and I know how much more my students could accomplish if I had that kind of support from more of their parents."

You need this kind of commitment from parents today. Parents are the most important people in a child's life. Their love, affection, support and approval are a fundamental need of all children. And because parents are #1 in importance, they are also #1 in the ability to influence and motivate their children.

The value of parent involvement and support has been thoroughly studied and evaluated by leading researchers in the educational community.

- A 1986 United States Department of Education study concluded that "the family is critical to success in school." Indeed, the "curriculum of the home" is twice as predictive of academic learning as family socioeconomic status . . .(and) parent influence is no less important in the high school years."[1]

- Noted researcher Urie Bronfenbrenner studied a number of educational intervention programs. He concluded that active involvement and support of the family are critical to a child's success in school.[2]

- R.J. Gigliotti and W.B. Brookover studied schools of similar size, geographic locale and student SES. They found that parent participation was a critical factor in determining the overall effectiveness of the schools, regardless of the economic level of the parents.[3]

- Joyce Epstein of Johns Hopkins University studied teachers who actively sought parent involvement. She found that there were positive changes in student achievement, attitude and behavior when teachers included parent involvement as part of their regular teaching practices. The students reported that they had a more positive attitude toward school and more regular home-work habits.[4]

- Anne T. Henderson summarized nearly 50 studies of parent involvement programs and concluded the following:

  - Programs designed with strong parent involvement components produced students who performed better than otherwise identical programs that did not strongly involve parents.

  - Schools that relate well to their communities have student bodies that outperform other schools.

  - Children whose parents help them at home and stay in touch with schools score higher than children of similar aptitude and family background whose parents are not involved. Schools in which children are failing im-proved dramatically when parents are called in to help.[5]

There is no doubt, the research shows, that when parents are involved and supportive, students benefit.

Teachers speak out for parent involvement.
A 1989 *Instructor* magazine poll asked educators to name the one thing they would like to tell national policymakers about the most effective way to raise student achievement. The answer given most frequently was "more parental involvement." These teachers went on

to state that they felt parental involvement was more important than smaller class size, more important than increased control and power for teachers, more important than promoting student responsibility and more important than decreasing the time students spend watching television.[6]

The *Instructor* poll was supported by the 1985 Gallup survey of teachers, which reported that over 90% did not feel they were getting the support they need from parents. The teachers listed lack of parental support as one of the top problems facing education today.[7]

You can get the support you need.
Parents of the 90s are anything but a homogeneous group. Their numbers include single mothers, single fathers, stepmothers, stepfathers, newly arrived immigrants, the affluent, the middle class, and an ever-increasing number of poverty-level parents.

These parents—and their situations—may differ in many ways. But in spite of their differences, they share something significant in common. Each and every one could be a positive factor in shaping the success of his or her children. Each and every one could provide the motivation that your students need to do their best in school. Parents are a resource that must be tapped and cultivated.

These parents—and their situations—may differ in many ways. But in spite of their differences, they share something significant in common.

An uninvolved parent, justifiably or not, gives a child the message that the child just isn't important enough to warrant close attention. An involved parent, on the other hand, can provide the boost to a student's self-esteem that will lead to greater success in school and a more fulfilling and accomplished adulthood.

> **❝** *Parent involvement isn't just a nice idea. For the sake of our children, it's essential.* **❞**

That's what this book is all about. *Parents On Your Side* is a step-by-step program developed to give you, the educator, the ability to work effectively with today's parents. You can't solve society's problems. You can't right all the wrongs. But you can learn how to communicate effectively with parents. Our practical approach will give you the skills and confidence you need to get all parents to support your academic, discipline and homework efforts. The approaches of the 50s, 60s and 70s will not work with today's parents. *Parents On Your Side* will help you work successfully with the parents of the 90s. The program is based on two important premises:

You can learn how to communicate effectively with parents.

Educators can get parents on their side.
There are teachers today who consistently receive support from all kinds of parents in all kinds of situations. We have studied these educators and found that there are common elements that are critical to their success. In *Parents On Your Side* you will learn the techniques that effective teachers use to work successfully with parents.

Parents want to support you.
The vast majority of parents of your students really do want to be involved. They do care about their children and want to provide needed support. In many cases, however, they just don't know what to do—or if they should do it at all. To put it into perspective, only 25% of parents report receiving systematic requests or directions from teachers on how they can help their children academically. However, when requested to give additional assistance, over 85% of parents immediately re-

The vast majority of parents of your students really do want to be involved.

---

6   Parents On Your Side

sponded and were willing to spend at least 15 minutes per day working with their children.[8] In short, when parents are contacted by skilled, trained teachers who communicate effectively, they will respond.

If students are to reach their full potential, they need the support and encouragement of an entire community of concerned, caring adults. That community includes all of us. And it especially includes student's parents. To do your job effectively, you need to get those parents on your side.

Parents On Your Side will show you how to get the support of parents. You will learn:

- how to develop an effective attitude toward parent involvement.

- how to recognize and move past the roadblocks that stand in your way.

- what to do before the school year starts.

- how to establish a yearlong positive parent communication program.

- how to involve parents in their children's homework.

- what to do when problems arise.

- how to contact a parent about a problem.

- how to use home-school contracts.

- how to develop a plan for conducting parent conferences.

- how to deal with difficult parents.

In Chapter 2 we'll begin by taking a look at the effective attitude shared by teachers who do get parent support.

References

[1] United States Department of Education (1986). *What Works: Research About Teaching and Learning.* Washington, D.C.

[2] Bronfenbrenner, Urie. (1966). *A Report on Longitudinal Evaluations of PreSchool Programs.* Washington, D.C.: Department of Health, Education and Welfare.

[3] Brookober, W.B. and Gigliotti, R.J. (1988). *First Teachers: Parental Involvement in the Public Schools.* Alexandria, VA: National School Boards Association.

[4] Epstein, J. (1983). *Effects on Parents of Teacher Practices in Parental Involvement.* Baltimore, OH: Johns Hopkins University Center for Social Organization of Schools.

[5] Henderson, A. (1987). *The Evidence Continues to Grow.* Columbia, Maryland: National Committee for Citizens in Education.

[6] Epstein, J. (1983). *Effects on Parents of Teacher Practices in Parental Involvement.* Baltimore, OH: Johns Hopkins University Center for Social Organization of Schools.

[7] Clapp, B. (1989). The Discipline Challenge. *Instructor,* Vol. XCIX (2), 32-34.

[8] Gallup, A. (1989). The Second Gallup/Phi Delta Kappa Survey of Public School Teacher Opinion. *Phi Delta Kappan,* 79 (No. 11).

Chapter 2
Effective Teachers — Effective Attitudes

> ❝ *Effective teachers don't just 'get' parents on their side, they have an attitude that enables them to work with parents.* ❞

The best way to learn how to get parents on your side is from teachers who already are successful at getting parent support. In researching this book, we studied teachers who consistently get the support they need from parents. We discovered that these teachers may differ greatly in where they teach, how they teach and whom they teach, but they do not differ at all in their attitude regarding parents.

These teachers share four important qualities:

- Effective teachers know they must have the support of parents.

- In every interaction with parents, effective teachers demonstrate their concern for the child.

- In all situations, effective teachers treat parents the way they would want to be treated.

- In every interaction with parents, effective teachers demonstrate professionalism and confidence.

Let's look more closely...

■ Effective teachers know they must have parent support.

Effective teachers understand, without a doubt, that when parents are involved, their students do better academically and behaviorally. Experience supports this conclusion. Research backs it up. But effective teachers take this knowledge one step further. As professionals responsible for the education of their students, these teachers believe that it is a dereliction of responsibility to allow a student to flounder academically or behaviorally without doing everything possible to help—and "help" means getting parents involved. Any lesser effort, in their view, would be "educational malpractice." Clearly, the belief in the right to parent support is basic to an effective teacher's perspective.

Effective teachers also unequivocally believe that they owe it to themselves to receive support from parents. Teachers are often faced with the responsibility of not only educating students but of helping solve their emotional and behavioral problems, too. It is not in anyone's best interest to struggle endlessly over student problems without the involvement of parents. It's emotionally draining, time consuming and ultimately non-productive.

For your students and for yourself, you must have parent support. Parents are in a unique position to deliver the help that is needed. Effective teachers recognize some basic truths about a parent's role in a child's life:

Parents are the most important, influential people in a child's life.

No one—teacher, principal, counselor or psychologist—can have as profound an impact on student behavior as can parents. Parental love and approval are fundamental needs of each and every child. All children want and need the praise and positive support of their parents.

Parental approval is a powerful motivator for students, one that can bring dramatic results. And yet parents may not be aware of the influence they have over their children, or how to use this influence to their best advantage. When necessary, you must be prepared to guide parents towards positive reinforcement techniques that will motivate their child to greater success in school.

Parents have the most time to work one-on-one with their child.

No matter how dedicated you are, you have a limited amount of time to work individually with students. For example, in a typical elementary classroom you may spend a maximum of five minutes per day giving students individual attention on their reading or math skills. When you can encourage a parent to spend 15 minutes a night helping a child, you are tripling the amount of individual attention that child can receive. Likewise, the one minute of personal attention a secondary teacher may be able to give a student could be increased as much as fifteenfold when the parent helps at home.

Encourage a parent to spend 15 minutes a night helping a child.

Parents can offer disciplinary backing.

Realistically, you are limited in what you can do when a student chooses to misbehave. Techniques such as time out, detention, and in-school suspension work for some students. There are, however, other students who need to know that parents will also follow through with disciplinary measures at home for misbehavior exhibited during the day. Students need to know that if they choose to misbehave in class, it's as if they are misbehaving in front of their parents. When misbehavior at school means loss of privileges at home, there is a much greater likelihood of a student's choosing to improve his or her behavior.

To illustrate more clearly, let's look at the parent involvement issue from the perspective of another group of professionals that deals with children—pediatricians:

The pediatrician knows that it is his or her responsibility to diagnose a child's problem, prescribe treatment, and carefully explain to parents what they must do to help their child. The pediatrician then fully expects that parents will support his or her efforts. If a parent complains that "I work, I can't make sure he takes his medicine," or "I'm too busy to get her to her checkup," the doctor will lay it on the line: "I cannot make sure your child gets better unless you do your part."

The issues that you deal with are every bit as immediate and important as those the pediatrician faces. Children who experience school failure have a higher probability of ending up on drugs, in jail or on welfare. These outcomes can be as serious as most physical problems a child will encounter, and you have every bit the right to parent backing as a doctor does. Remember, teachers and doctors are both professionals responsible for the well-being and growth of a child.

In every interaction with parents, effective teachers demonstrate concern for students.

A great concern of parents is that their child's teacher will not put in the time and effort necessary to ensure that their child succeeds in school. Effective teachers know this and take steps to alleviate these parental worries. Experience has shown them that when a parent believes that a teacher really cares about their child, that parent is not as likely to argue, make excuses or question the teacher's competency. Instead, the parent will make every effort to support the teacher.

Here are some strategies that effective teachers use to demonstrate concern for their students:

From the beginning of the school year, communicate your concern.

It is never too early to show parents you care. Some teachers begin even before the school year starts. A welcoming phone call or note home to parents of incoming students can go a long way toward demonstrating your interest in their child.

Establish positive communication with parents.

The key to showing genuine concern is to contact parents when the child is doing something right. When parents hear good news, it's easier for them to believe that you really do care. You will also find that once you've established positive communication with parents, they will be much more receptive when you have to call them with a problem.

Most parents report that they only hear from the teacher when there is a problem. When every communication is negative, it's easy to understand why parents avoid contact with teachers. After all, most parents would like to believe that their child is doing something right at school, at least some of the time. In Chapter 6 we will be looking at a variety of ways to communicate with parents in positive ways.

Take every opportunity to show you care.

In every interaction with parents, all eyes are on you. Don't miss any opportunity to let parents know that you care about their child. Failure to show concern may miscommunicate to the parent a lack of caring on your part. From the start, look for occasions that will show your interest and concern. Notes home, phone calls, birthday greetings and get-well cards not only address the occasion but also consistently demonstrate to parents that your commitment to their child is genuine.

◥ Effective teachers treat parents the way they would want to be treated.

Teachers who are most successful in getting parent support adhere to the "golden rule" of positive parent relations: Treat parents the way you would want to be treated if you had a child in school. This common-sense approach to positive parent involvement is one of the most valuable qualities you can develop.

By following this golden rule, you will gain two important advantages:

First, through your words and actions, you will consistently demonstrate to parents that you are a concerned and caring teacher. Your underlying message at all times will be, "I understand your needs and I will be sensitive to them."

Second, you will have a guideline for determining how you will approach and deal with parents in all situations. When you ask yourself, What would I as a parent want to see happen in this situation, the answer will usually be surprisingly clear.

For example:

- If I had a child in school, what specific information would I want to hear from the teacher at the beginning of the year?
- How and when would I want to be approached about a problem?
- How would I want to be spoken to?
- How would I want to listened to?
- Would I like to hear from the teacher when my child is doing well or only when there is a problem?

Putting yourself in the parent's place can take the guesswork out of determining how to handle many situations. You will find the golden rule mentioned throughout *Parents On Your Side* because it is the guiding force behind many of the techniques and suggestions given. Keep it in mind because it applies to each and every issue discussed.

Effective teachers demonstrate professionalism and confidence.

You can be the most skilled teacher in the world, but if parents don't recognize your competence you'll have a difficult time getting their support. What can you do to demonstrate your professionalism and let parents know you have confidence in your ability?

Involve parents.

A confident teacher welcomes the support and involvement of parents and is not intimidated by the help a parent can offer. A confident teacher views education as a team effort, and parents as a part of that team.

Professionalism in dealing with parents requires that you have a plan for working with parents all year long. Parent involvement is not a twice-a-year event. It is a daily part of your responsibilities. It cannot be left to chance encounters and sporadic conversations. You need to know exactly when, how and why you will contact parents from the first day of school to the last. You need to develop a parent involvement plan.

A parent involvement plan is your plan of action for dealing with parents throughout the year. This plan is not a strict, step-by-step prescription. A successful parent involvement plan is one that you develop to meet your specific needs, and the needs of your students and their parents. In the following chapters you will find the practical techniques that you can use to get and keep parent support—in all situations, at all grade levels and with all kinds of parents. These techniques will be your guide for developing a plan of your own.

Develop a parent involvement plan.

Demonstrate.

Show your confidence in every interaction with parents. Each time you meet with a parent, speak on the phone or send a note home, you have a new opportunity to shine. Make the most of these opportunities. Stop and think a minute before you speak or write a note. Be professional, confident and assertive. Then let your words and attitude carry that message forth.

Communicate.

Assured communication—communication that says "I know what I'm doing" —is vital to working effectively with parents. Would you hire an attorney who vacillated on how to advise you? Why should a parent be expected to support a teacher who does not appear to have confidence in his or her abilities? You have to impress upon parents that you do in fact know what you're doing. You have to learn to project the attitude of self-assurance that earns respect and promotes confidence. That means learning communication skills.

In Chapter 3 we will look at some of the roadblocks that keep parents and teachers from communicating effectively.

Recognizing Roadblocks **3**

> **"** *It takes two to communicate, but it's up to you to keep the path of communication clear and open.* **"**

Successful parent involvement depends upon your ability to get your message across to all parents in all kinds of situations. To do so, you must learn to recognize and move past the communication road-blocks that may stand in your way. As a teacher, you are faced with two types of roadblocks:

• Roadblocks that keep teachers from initiating communication.

• Roadblocks that keep parents from giving support.

▱ Teachers' Roadblocks

In Chapter 2, we looked at the ways teachers develop and maintain an effective attitude when working with parents. This attitude, however, is only as effective as the teacher's ability to communicate it:

- If you find yourself doubting whether or not it is your responsibility to handle a problem situation, you may find yourself on unsure ground when you try to solve it.

- If you feel you've never been trained to work with parents, then you may find yourself stumbling over your own words and actions.

- If you have negative feelings about working with parents in general, it can easily appear as a lack of confidence and competence.

Let's look at these three types of roadblocks that often prevent teachers from asking for the help they need from parents:

Teachers' Roadblock #1:
The Myth of the "Good Teacher"

"Our district wants parents happy at all costs. We are basically told to handle problems on our own. If we go to parents for help, they'll think we don't know what we're doing."

"Everyone expects us to handle problems with our students on our own. It's a clear message at this school that if you have to involve parents, the administration thinks you're not up to snuff."

Over the last 20 years, many schools and school districts have developed the attitude that competent teachers should handle all of their students' problems on their own, without the help of parents. We can call this the myth of the "good teacher." Many administrators have fostered this myth by discouraging teachers from contacting parents when problems arise. Many parents have fostered this myth by responding in a negative manner when teachers call. The underlying assumption seemed to be that teachers should handle it all by themselves, that it is not "professional" to involve parents.

Do you do any of these?

- Wait until the last minute before calling a parent about a problem?

- Avoid talking to parents because you are afraid they will judge you?

- Apologize to parents when you do speak with them?

- Negate problems?

- Avoid talking with your administrator about problems you are having with students or parents?

If you answered yes to any of these questions, you, too, probably buy into the myth of the good teacher. This is important for you to recognize. If you really feel less than professional when you need to work with parents, it is reflected in how you speak and act. You will present yourself to others not as a competent and confident professional, but as an unsure, faltering novice.

Here's an example of how the myth of the good teacher can creep into a phone conversation between parent and teacher:

The conversation begins with an apology.

Teacher: I'm really sorry to bother you at home. I know how busy you are.

The teacher then proceeds to belittle her own abilities.

Teacher: I really just don't know what to do with Sara. She had problems again today, and I guess I don't know what else to try with her.

The teacher minimizes the severity of the problem.

Teacher: Sara hit another student today. Well, she didn't really
                  hurt her.

The teacher continues in an ineffectual way to ask for support.

Teacher: As I said, I'm not too sure what to do this time. I know
                  you've got six other kids and plenty of problems of
                  your own, but if you have the time I'd really appreciate
                  it if you'd have a word with Sara.

An uncertain attitude, together with a weak communication style, are
two reasons why teachers do not get parents on their side. Let's look
more closely at what went on in that conversation.

First, this teacher, like many teachers, began a parent conversation
by apologizing. There is no reason to apologize! Apologies are
given when you feel you have done something wrong. You are
calling the parent not to bother him or her but to discuss what can
be done to help the child. Making this call is your job and your
responsibility.

Second, this teacher belittled her own professional abilities. Teachers often say things to parents such as "I don't know what to do with
him (her)." Such statements do not exude confidence or professionalism. Instead, these statements lead par-
ents to believe that you are incompetent

*This teacher
belittled her own
professional
abilities.*

and incapable of handling their child. Obviously this can be frustrating to parents,
especially those with children who have
problems.

Let's return to the pediatrician analogy. Assume that your own child
is ill. You take your child to the doctor, who runs some tests and calls
you back the next day. She says to you,

> "I'm really sorry to bother you at home. I know how busy
> you are. I have the tests back and I'm really not sure what
> is going on with your child, but I think she has some kind

of bacterial infection. As I said, I know you're busy, but if you could find the time I'd really appreciate it if you'd go to the pharmacy and get your child some penicillin. Okay?"

This is an exaggerated example, but think about it for a moment. How would you feel about this doctor? Would you ever take your child back to see her? Would you have any confidence in this doctor? Would you support this doctor? The answers are no. But this is exactly the situation going on today with many teachers. They do not know what to say. They do not know how to say it. They are so tied up in the myth of the good teacher that they do not feel they have the right to ask for parent support. This attitude is reflected in everything they say to parents. Keep the pediatrician analogy in mind as you continue to read through this book. You will find that the analogy is pertinent to many of your professional situations.

The myth of the good teacher keeps too many teachers who really are good at everything else they do from working effectively with parents. Does this roadblock apply to you? If so, you must learn to overcome it if you are going to establish support from parents. We will give you the techniques and confidence to get past this roadblock.

Teachers' Roadblock #2:
Negative Expectations About Working with Parents

"You can't reach parents, and if you do, all you hear is that they don't know what to do and they want you to handle the problem. Why bother trying to work with them?"

Nonproductive encounters with parents can lead teachers to develop negative expections about the support they can get from parents. These negative expectations can then easily lead to negative feelings about working with parents at all. When this happens, parent contact quickly breaks down, often resulting in a parent being called only as a last resort, when a problem is totally out of hand or at a crisis state.

Consider this situation: A group of middle school teachers were having academic and behavioral problems with a large number of their students. Upon examination of their grade books, it was apparent that there were students who had not completed an assignment for weeks. Other students had been given 5 to 10 detentions. When asked what contact they had had with parents, the teachers responded that not one of them had called a parent. When asked why parents had not been contacted, one teacher summed up the attitude of the others: "The parents in this area don't back us up and don't care. They want us to not only educate the children but raise them too!" These teachers felt that there was no value in taking the time and effort to work with their students' parents.

Parents don't back us up and don't care.

A teacher's negative expectations are often a direct result of having been questioned and criticized by parents. Many teachers say that the most stressful part of their job is working with angry, critical parents. When a teacher has had several unproductive conferences with hostile parents, is subjected to parents who threaten to sue or go to the school board, or is threatened with bodily harm, it is easy to understand why he or she might become defensive and anxious.

The negativity educators sometimes feel towards parents can be a major roadblock to getting parents on your side. Remember, negative expectations are based on past experiences. Tomorrow is new. Armed with skills and techniques for dealing with parents, you can get past this roadblock.

Teachers' Roadblock #3:
Lack of Training in Working with Parents

"I know that I avoid dealing with parents. I'm not comfortable working with parents. I know how to work with kids; I don't know how to work with parents."

"I was trained to do one thing—teach children. Parents were not even mentioned in my education classes."

Do you find that you avoid dealing with parents because you're just not comfortable working with them? You're not alone. Most teachers will agree that they were trained to teach students and that parents were never even mentioned in their education classes.

Teachers know they need training in working with parents if they are to do their job effectively. In a recent survey, almost 87% of teachers indicated that they felt they should be trained how to work with parents. Over 73% of teachers felt this training should be required in their undergraduate program. Principals felt this training was even more important. 92% felt teachers should be trained to work with parents and 83% of principals felt this training should be required.

Given the perceived need for training, what is provided in a typical teacher education program? A recent study indicates that only 37% of education programs provided as much as one class period on how to work with parents[1] In the vast majority of all teacher education classes there is, for all intents and purposes, no content focusing on this issue.

In the past, teachers did not need this training. In most instances a phone call home could solve a problem. Teachers asked for help and parents followed through. The situation has changed today. Without training, you may find that you do not have the skills and confidence necessary to get the backing you need from parents.

Just as you need to know how to develop lesson plans for curriculum and create a discipline plan for behavior management, you also need to know how to work with parents. This requires special skills. You must be trained to work with all kinds of parents, including those who question or challenge your professional competence.

Working with parents requires special skills.

To accomplish this, you must learn to listen effectively—and respond accordingly. A teacher, just as any business manager, needs to be trained in effective communication skills.

▥ Parents' Roadblocks

The roadblocks aren't all yours. Parents have roadblocks of their own that keep them from giving support. Learn to listen. Pinpointing the type of roadblock a parent might be focused on will enable you to use specific techniques to move the parent past the roadblock and get the support you need.

We have identified four parent roadblocks that typically keep parents from backing you. As you consider each of these, keep in mind that by recognizing the roadblock, a teacher's response can direct the ensuing conversation to a productive conclusion.

Parents' Roadblock #1:
Parents Are Overwhelmed

> *"Ever since my divorce, my life has fallen apart. Sometimes I just don't feel like I can make it on my own raising a family. I know I should discipline my sons to behave at school, but really, I'd just rather the teacher handle it, because I can't cope."*

When you hear a parent make comments like these, you need to know that you're dealing with a parent who is overwhelmed, that this parent is coping with a stressful situation in his or her life. Armed with this information, you can gear your response to moving the parent past this roadblock and avoid getting bogged down in a conversation that accomplishes nothing.

The term "at-risk student" is very popular today. We could coin another term, "at-risk parent." These are parents who are at risk of being overwhelmed by the stress in their lives. They do not feel they have the time or energy to support their childrens' education to the degree necessary to ensure their children's success.

You will find at-risk parents in all kinds of households. While it's true that many at-risk parents are part of the growing population of single parents struggling to raise and support a family on their own, it's also true that at-risk parents can be found in the most affluent two-parent homes. The point is, there can be many reasons why parents are overwhelmed with their lives: poverty, divorce, illness, or job stress. These parents may feel that school is the last thing they have the time or energy to deal with. Overwhelmed parents are a very real roadblock to getting the support you need.

Learn to actively listen to what a parent is saying.

To get past this roadblock, you need to learn to actively listen to what a parent is saying to you—and react appropriately. Listen for words or phrases that will cue you to a parent's state of mind.

The scene: The teacher calls a parent regarding a homework problem. She introduces herself and begins discussing the problem with the parent. Before she gets very far, the parent interjects the following comments:

Parent: I hear what you're saying, but I come home so tired at night, the last thing in the world I can do is battle with my child over homework. I know he should do it, and I know I'm the one who should be making sure he does it. But I'm just too tired to deal with it.

Here are two ways a teacher could respond:

Teacher A: Mrs. Jones, Eddie has to turn in all of his homework assignments or he's going to fail this class. That's all there is to it. I don't want that to happen and, I'm sure, neither do you.

Teacher B: I hear how difficult it is for you now. I also hear you saying that you really are concerned about how your son does in school. Mrs. Jones, we both want success for him. I'm here to work with you to see that happens. I'm going to give you some suggestions that will help you check on his homework progress each night easily and quickly.

• Teacher A failed to notice the parent's roadblock and consequently will probably end up without the support she needs to solve the problem.

• Teacher B has recognized that she is dealing with an overwhelmed parent. She knows that if she doesn't help move the parent past this roadblock, she won't get the support she needs. This teacher listened and heard. She recognized that the parent was not uncaring or hostile, but overwhelmed. She therefore adjusted her response to lead the conversation in a direction that would not cause the parent anxiety and add to her burden. Chances are good that this teacher will get the support she needs from this parent. And that means the student will get the help he needs.

Parents' Roadblock #2:
Parents Want to Help but Don't Know How

"I tell her to study. I tell her to do her homework. She says she will and then she just doesn't do it. I have no idea how to get through to this kid."

This is a parent who cares, but doesn't know what to do. Each year you will encounter parents who do not have the strength and/or skills needed to motivate their children to perform academically or behave appropriately in school or at home. And if parents cannot get their children to behave at home, it's not likely that they will be able to give you the support you need to ensure that their children behave in school. These are parents who need and often will accept your help. They want their children to succeed as much as you do. It is your responsibility to recognize this roadblock and to get help to them.

These are the parents who will be eager to become actively involved.

Learn to recognize this roadblock because very often these are the parents who, with guidance and support, will be eager to become actively involved in their child's education.

The scene: A teacher is meeting with a parent about a behavior problem. As the teacher begins discussing the problem, the parent responds:

Parent: Believe me, I'd do something if I could. I know how John behaves at school is wrong; he's the same way at home. I just don't have any idea what to do to help him stop. And what difference would it make anyway? He doesn't listen to a thing I say.

Here are two possible responses:

Teacher A: Well, John needs to behave at school. I can't have him disrupting my class.

Teacher B: I hear you saying that you really want to help John learn to behave at school. And I know it's not always easy to know how to do it. If you'd like, we can work together to come up with some solutions. I've worked with lots of kids just like John. I can promise you that if we put our heads together, we will come up with some solutions that will get John back on track.

• Teacher A has pushed the problem, not a solution, onto the parent. If he had listened more effectively, he would have heard that the parent is really at a loss for what to do.

• Teacher B realized that she was speaking with a parent who was willing to help but just didn't have any idea what to do. Knowing she had to move the parent past this roadblock, she responded by offering further suggestions for what the parent could do to remedy the problem. Through her words, this teacher let the parent know that she was concerned enough about the student to take the time to help solve the problem.

Parents' Roadblock #3:
Parents' Negative Feelings About School

"I hated school. I never even graduated. The teachers were always on my case and now they're on my son's case."

Each year you will encounter parents who themselves had negative school experiences. Often when a parent did not perform well academically, was constantly in trouble and/or dropped out of school, he or she harbors negative feelings about school in general and teachers in particular. These parents often do not trust teachers and may feel that teachers do not have their children's best interests at heart. Since these parents had negative experiences in school, they tend to avoid involvement in school activities. It is often difficult to get them to come to Back-to-School Night, parent conferences, school performances and other events.

Finally, these parents may actually expect their children to have academic or behavioral problems in school just like they did. Their own experiences may lead them to believe that this is just how children behave in school. Thus, these parents tend to feel there is no reason to get involved in solving their child's problems because there is nothing that really can be done about them.

Because a parent's negative attitude can easily be transferred to the child, it is important to recognize this roadblock and take steps to get these parents positively involved.

The scene: The teacher calls a parent to discuss an academic problem. As soon as the teacher begins to speak, the parent goes on the offensive:

Parent: You teachers today don't like kids any more than my teachers did. All you ever do is call me and tell me how bad my kids are."

Here are two possible responses:

Teacher A: Mr. Smith, I'm calling because your son isn't performing as he should in my class.

Teacher B: Mr. Smith, I'm much more interested in calling you to let you know about how terrific your son is. And he is a terrific kid. That's why it's so important that we both work together to solve this problem. Your son can be doing a lot better in class. I want to see that happen. I care about your son's success, and I know you do, too.

• Teacher A ignored the parent's roadblock and continued to address his original agenda. Ignoring the parent's anger won't diffuse it. The conversation will probably lead to a dead end. The parent will still be hostile and the teacher will still not have support.

• Teacher B determined that he was speaking with a parent who had strong negative feelings about teachers and school in general. He knew that this parent would never listen to anything until this roadblock was removed. The teacher let this parent know that he in fact was dealing with a teacher who does care.

Parents' Roadblock #4:
Parents' Negative View of Teacher Competence

"Schools have gone downhill. I know it. Everyone in the neighborhood knows it. I'm not going to stand by and let my child's teacher ruin his school experience."

From time to time you will encounter parents who simply do not respect your professional expertise. There are several reasons why this is so. First, hardly a week goes by that there isn't media attention focusing on the "dismal" state of the American educational system, focusing in particular on the poor performance of students. In many instances the blame is placed on the teachers. It seems as though teacher bashing is in vogue in America today. Parents cannot help but absorb this constant negativity regarding the educational system their children are involved in.

Second, there are more parents today with a higher level of educational sophistication than ever before. Many of these parents have their own theories of how their child should be educated and will not hesitate to state these opinions, valid or invalid, to the teacher.

Third, there are, unfortunately, still some teachers who are not competent enough to meet the needs of students. The inability of the educational system to remove these teachers has added tremendous fuel to the fire of parental discontent. All it takes is one incompetent teacher in a building to stir the wrath of parents. When these teachers are not removed, the frustration level of parents and colleagues increases and an entire school can be labeled inadequate.

All it takes is one incompetent teacher in a building to stir the wrath of parents.

Keep in mind that negative views of a teacher's competence can come across in many forms, from outright hostility to subtle questioning. To diffuse this negativity, you need to really listen to what a parent is saying, not just react defensively or in anger.

The scene: The parent calls the teacher about a low grade her daughter has earned.

Parent: My child is special and I want a teacher who can meet her special needs. I will not sit by and settle for anything less.

Here are two possible responses:

Teacher A: I'm doing the best I can with her.

Teacher B: You're right to want the best for your child. That's why
I want to work with you to see that she is successful in
my class.

• Teacher A let the parent get to her. She was probably hurt and
became defensive. Her weak response will only make the parent
angrier and feel more justified about her assumptions. The teacher's
response certainly will not increase the parent's confidence in her.

• Teacher B knows she is listening to a parent who has a negative
attitude regarding teacher competence. And she knows that reactionary responses will get her nowhere. She therefore demonstrates
strength, assurance and confidence in her ability.

Why listen for parents' roadblocks?

As the sample scenes with parents illustrate, by listening for
parents' roadblocks, and responding accordingly, a teacher can
open communication and bring parents and teachers together to
solve problems.

It's a matter of sensitivity—of taking the time to think about what a
parent is really saying to you. You can't do your best for your students
without the support of their parents. And parents can't give that
support if they are focused on anger, confusion or or any other roadblock. Moving each and every conversation with parents forward to
a productive conclusion is the way to get parents on your side.

As you read through this book, notice that
in all scripted verbal exchanges between
parent and teacher, the teacher asks for
and listens to parent input. By doing so, the
teacher demonstrates to the parent that he

*The teacher asks
for and listens to
parent input.*

---

or she cares about the parent's point of view. Hearing what is said, and adjusting your responses accordingly, is the foundation of effective communication.

Recognizing the roadblocks that stand in your way is an important step to getting parents on your side. You are making a diagnosis. Once you recognize a specific problem you can start taking steps to remedy it.

Reference

[1] Chavkin, N.F., and Williams, D.L., Jr. (1988) "Critical Issues in Teacher Training for Parent Involvement." *Educational Horizons*, vol.66, pp 87-89.

All Kinds of Families

The key to parent involvement is communication. The key to successful communication is awareness and sensitivity.

A teacher today works with many kinds of families, including stepfamilies, single-parent and two-parent families, families torn by poverty or wrestling with divorce, transient families and non-English speaking families.

Today, a teacher can't assume that one method or style of communication will fit the needs of all. An effective teacher must at all times be sensitive to the varying realities of the families of his or her students.

Throughout *Parents On Your Side* you are given a wide variety of parent communication suggestions. Before you put any of these to use, take time to think about the person with whom you will be communicating. Make every effort to satisfy yourself that you are, to the best of your ability, communicating in an appropriate manner.

Take special care to be aware of the cultural diversity of your students and make every effort to gain an understanding of their varying cultural expectations and values. Let that knowledge guide your words and actions throughout the year. What are acceptable behaviors, or manners, in one culture may not be in another.

Your professional judgment must lead you as you communicate with each and every parent. Keep this thought in mind as you continue to read *Parents On Your Side*, and as you begin to implement the program into your own teaching routine.

Chapter 4
First-Day Objectives

> **"** *Parent contact needs to
> begin before the first day of school.* **"**

Start working as soon as possible to get the parent support you need. It's up to you to make the first move, to clearly communicate to parents the value and necessity of their involvement and support. Don't wait until a problem comes up. Don't wait for them to come to you. Reach out to them, right away. Parent contact needs to begin before the first day of school.

The first actions you take will quickly help to establish your reputation with parents as an effective professional who not only cares about the welfare of their children, but who also has the confidence and skill to take charge. Set immediate objectives for yourself and take the actions that will achieve them. The purpose of meeting these objectives is to break down communication barriers, get past roadblocks, and set the stage for productive interaction all year long.

First-Day Objectives

Here are three objectives to meet on or before the first day of school:

- Send a "before school starts" greeting to all parents and incoming students.

- Open up verbal communication with parents of potential problem students.

- Communicate your expectations to parents.

Parents On Your Side

■ Send a "before school starts" greeting to all parents and incoming students.

Before the beginning of the school year, you are probably unknown to most of your students' parents, and perhaps to the students themselves. Introduce yourself by saying a friendly hello. Take time during vacation—before school starts—to drop a line to incoming students and their parents. You don't need to say much, just let them know that you're enthusiastic about the upcoming year.

Dear Mr. and Mrs. Robinson:

Just a quick note to let you know I'm looking forward to working with Karen this year, and to getting to know both of you. Please feel free to drop by the classroom on the first day of school, September 10. I'd like to say hello!

Sincerely,

Miss Warner

Dear Karen:

Welcome to Room 14! I'm looking forward to a terrific year and I hope you are, too. Enjoy the rest of your vacation. I'll see you September 10.

Sincerely,

Miss Warner

Sample "before school starts" greetings

These brief notes are a preview of the many positive communications parents and students will be receiving from you throughout the year.

Open up verbal communication with parents of potential problem students.

Have you been assigned students who have a history of problems in school? Don't just complain about it in the teacher's room. Do something positive about it! Take some constructive actions to get the parents of these students on your side now by calling the parents before school begins.

The goal of your conversation is to establish positive communication.

The goal of your conversation is to establish positive communication and to reassure parents of your concern, professionalism and confidence in your ability to work with their child. Remember, these parents are probably used to hearing from school only when there is a problem. Here's your chance to make a difference and show them that you are a concerned teacher. You are going to turn this situation around and contact them with good news. You'll let them know that you are confident that you and they can work together to make this a successful year for their child. What a welcome message that will be!

Here's your chance to show them that you are a concerned teacher.

Plan before you dial.

Before making the call, write down all the points you want to cover with the parent, then keep your notes with you as you speak. Your preparatory efforts will be well worth it. If you deal effectively with this first phone call, you will probably have far greater support from this parent throughout the year.

Plan to address each of these points:

1. Begin with a statement of concern.
The first words you speak will set the tone for the entire conversation. Be sensitive to the parent's feelings. Keep in mind that the last thing he or she wants to hear are problems concerning the child—before the school year has even begun! You have to let this parent know up front that you are calling out of concern for the child and a sincere desire to make the new year a success.

"Mrs. Jones, this is Mrs. Williams. I'm going to be Bobby's fifth-grade teacher. I wanted to speak to you before the school year began because I want to make sure that this year is a successful one for your child."

2. Get parental input concerning the problems of last year.

Demonstrate your concern for the parent's point of view. Let the parent know that you genuinely care how he or she feels about what happened the previous year. This is the time to listen for roadblocks. Is the parent overwhelmed? Angry? Unable to deal with the child's problems? Gear your response to what the parent says to you.

"I would like to know your view of what Bobby's experience at school was last year."

3. Get parental input for what will be needed to make this year more successful.

Listen to the parent's suggestions. He or she may be able to offer valuable insights that will help you get off to a better start with the student. The information may give you an advantage in dealing with the student from the first day.

"I'd like to know what you feel we need to do to insure Bobby has a good year this year."

4. Explain that parent support is critical.

Let the parent know how important his or her support is.

"I believe that you can help me with Bobby. I will be in touch with you throughout the year because your support is vital. You are the most important person in your child's life and Bobby must know that we are working together to help him."

5. Express your confidence.

Put yourself in this parent's position. Another school year is starting. If it's anything like the last, it may be a continual round of negative feedback from school. Give the parent something to be optimistic about! The confidence you project will encourage the parent to give the support you need.

"I have complete confidence that by working together we will help Bobby to have a good year. I want to assure you that I've worked with many children like Bobby before, and I am certain I can make this year a great year for your son."

Here's a sample elementary level conversation:

Parent: Hello.

Teacher: Mrs. Smith?

Parent: Yes.

Teacher: This is Mrs. Lawrence. I'll be Ted's teacher next year *(introduce yourself)*.

Parent: Oh, hello.

Teacher: The reason I'm calling *(state reason)* is that I'm working to make sure that this year is a successful one for Ted.

Parent: I'm glad to hear that. Last year wasn't very good for Ted at all.

Teacher: Can you tell me why you feel it was not good *(get parental input)*?

Parent: Oh, I don't know. The teacher and Ted didn't get along. She was very negative. They had what I guess you would call a personality conflict. I felt she didn't know how to handle him and then she would call me and expect me to do her job. You know, she's the teacher and she should handle some of those things. I sure didn't know what to do.

Teacher: I understand last year was very frustrating for you. I'd really like to hear any suggestions you might have that could help Ted have a better year this year *(get parental suggestion for solution)*.

Parent: My son needs a lot of attention. He's had a tough couple of years. Ever since my husband and I got divorced, Ted has not been motivated. He just doesn't care or do his best work. But I really feel no teacher has given him the attention and support he needs.

Teacher: I understand what you're saying, and let me assure you that I will make it a positive, supportive year for him. In fact, I've got an idea of something we can do right at the start of the year. Every day, I have a special monitor in class, and I think it would be great if for the first few days of school Ted is my special monitor. That will enable me to give him a lot of positive attention and support and make sure the first few days this year are really positive for him.

Parent: That may help. It's more than the teacher did last year.

Teacher: There's something else I know will help Ted *(parental support needed)*. That's the two of us working together this year. I absolutely believe that parents and teachers working together can ensure success for children.

Parent: I don't have much time. You know I work full time and have two other children.

Teacher: I understand. What I'm suggesting is not going to take a lot of time, but it can get results. Throughout the year I will give you ideas on how you can help Ted in a quick, positive way. You know, you are the most important person in Ted's life, and Ted must know we're working together to help him.

Parent: I see what you're saying, but I haven't had much success in the past with him.

Teacher:	I know how frustrating it can be with children, but let me assure you that I've worked with many students like Ted. And I've worked with many of their parents and have had great success. I am going to make it a point to see that Ted has a super year. I want Ted to like school and I want him to be a success.
Parent:	You sound like you mean it.
Teacher:	I do. I mean what I say.
Parent:	I really appreciate you taking the time to call. No teacher has ever done this before.
Teacher:	It's my pleasure. I will be in touch with you throughout the year and I want you to stay in touch with me. Before I say goodbye, I think it would help if I could speak to Ted for a few minutes to introduce myself to him and share my feelings about this year *(speak to child)*.

Here's a sample secondary level conversation:

Parent:	Hello.
Teacher:	Mrs. Greenfield?
Parent:	Yes.
Teacher:	This is Mr. Schwartz. I'll be your daughter Gail's social studies teacher next year. The reason I'm calling *(state reason)* is that I recently went through her school records and it appears she had a lot of trouble with social studies last year. I'd like to find out why she had these problems and what we can do to make sure they don't occur this year *(get parental input)*.
Parent:	Well I think I can tell you what the problem was. I think she has a poor attitude towards school.
Teacher:	I hear what you're saying. Can you tell me specifically what happened last year with her schoolwork?

Parent: Sometimes she told me she didn't have any homework when she really did. Then when she did do it, she didn't take any care and would race through it. She'd do it while she was on the phone with the stereo blasting or the TV on.

Teacher: I hear how hard it was last year. Do you have any suggestions about what I can do to help the situation this year *(get parental suggestion for solution)*?

Parent: I really don't know. To be honest, she probably needs a new group of friends. The kids she hangs out with are no good.

Teacher: I can't get her new friends, but I think maybe there are some things I can do as her teacher to help.

Parent: Well, she says she never believes that teachers really care. She always says that teachers could care less if she comes to class, or if she does her work or doesn't do her work. It never matters.

Teacher: Well, I'm a teacher who does care. I'll make sure she know that.

Parent: I don't know. She hasn't liked teachers and she hasn't liked school since the seventh grade. She's really been lost. Just lost.

Teacher: I think lots of kids get lost today in schools our size. I don't want her to get lost. That's why I'm calling. I want to work with her to make sure she is involved, does her classwork, and does her homework.

Parent: She needs a lot of help. She has no idea how to study.

Teacher: I can help her there. I can teach her some very simple, basic homework study skills that will enable her to be a lot more successful. There's a point I have to make, though. I will do my part, but I'm going to need your help if we are going to turn things around for Gail *(parental support needed)*.

Parent:	But she doesn't listen to me. I'm not even usually home when she does her homework. I'm at work and I don't know what I can do from there.
Teacher:	I don't want you to worry. I've worked with many students like your daughter. I've also worked with many parents in your position and let me assure you, we can help her. Throughout the year I'll give you guidelines and techniques that will help Gail study more successfully. I'll follow through at school, and you can follow through at home. How does that sound?
Parent:	I really appreciate your attitude. But I still don't know if it will do any good.
Teacher:	I know it will. We will work together. We will help your daughter. She is going to succeed in my class. With me doing my part and you doing your part, it will work. You can count on me. I will be behind you 100%.

Communicate your expectations to parents.

If they are to be actively involved, parents need some basic information right at the beginning of the school year. First, they need to know a little bit about you. After all, you are going to be an influential person in your students' lives. It's important that parents have an opportunity to know something more about you than your name and room number.

Secondly, parents of both elementary and secondary students need to know the teacher's classroom rules and standards. Think a minute about the parent contacts you have had in the past. What precipitated many of these contacts? Chances are it was either a behavior problem or a homework problem. These are, after all, the day-to-day problems that you deal with most often. It is, therefore, extremely important that you communicate to parents your standards and policies for

You can't ask parents to back up your rules if they don't know them.

both areas. You can't ask parents to back up your rules if they don't know them. Before school begins, you should formulate both a classroom discipline plan and a homework policy.

Send home the following on the first day of school:

• a letter of introduction

• a copy of your discipline plan

• a copy of your homework policy

Letter of Introduction
Give parents an opportunity to know something about you and your plans for the upcoming year.

• Keep your letter brief; no more than one page.

• The tone of your letter should be upbeat and enthusiastic.

• Take this opportunity to tell parents that you need their support, that the education of their children is a team effort.

• Above all, end the letter with a statement expressing your confidence in the success you expect for all of your students this year.

Dear Parents,

My name is Mrs. Mitchell, and I will be your child's fifth-grade teacher this year. I'm looking forward to an exciting, productive year working with you and your child.

Throughout my years of teaching, I have become committed to the importance of parent involvement in a student's education. I firmly believe that your child receives the best education possible when you and I work as a team.

Enclosed with this letter are copies of my classroom discipline plan and my homework policy. Please read both of these carefully. They explain many of my expectations for your child in this class. I need your support of these expectations, and I need you to let your child know also that you support these classroom rules and standards.

I will be keeping in close touch with you all year long. Please do the same with me. I welcome your calls and messages. Any time you have anything you'd like to discuss with me, please call the school office at 555-2222. I will return your call as quickly as possible.

I look forward to meeting you at Back-to-School Night on September 24. It's going to be an exciting evening that I know you won't want to miss.

Sincerely,

Mrs. Mitchell

Sample letter of introduction to parents

Your Classroom Discipline Plan

A classroom discipline plan is a system that allows you to clarify what behaviors you expect from students and what they can expect from you in return. The goal of a classroom discipline plan is to have a fair and consistent way in which to deal with all students who misbehave, thereby creating an atmosphere conducive to teaching and allowing more time on-task for learning.

A classroom discipline plan is an integral part of any teacher's parent involvement plan because it lets parents know exactly how their children are to behave, what will happen when they do behave and what will happen when they don't.

A classroom discipline plan consists of three parts:

1 **Rules** that students must follow at all times.

2 **Consequences** that result when students choose not to follow the rules.

3 **Rewards** for when students do follow the rules.

On the following pages are examples of classroom discipline plans for an elementary classroom and a secondary classroom.

Classroom Discipline Plan

Classroom Rules

- Follow directions.
- Keep hands, feet, objects to yourself.
- No teasing or name calling.
- Do not leave the room without permission.

Consequences

First time a student breaks a rule:	Warning
Second time:	Last in line for lunch
Third time:	Time-out area
Fourth time:	Teacher calls parents
Fifth time:	Send to principal
Severe Clause	Send to principal

Rewards

Students who comply with the rules receive:

- Praise
- Positive notes sent home
- Small rewards
- Class parties

Sample elementary discipline plan

Classroom Discipline Plan

Classroom Rules
- Follow directions.
- Be in the classroom and seated when the bell rings.
- Bring all appropriate materials to class.
- Keep hands, feet, objects to yourself.
- Do not swear.

Consequences

First time a student breaks a rule:	Warning
Second time:	Stays in class 1 minute after the bell
Third time:	Stays in class 2 minutes after the bell
Fourth time:	Call parents
Fifth time:	Send to principal
Severe Clause	Send to principal

Rewards
Students who comply with the rules receive:
- Praise
- Positive notes sent home
- Privilege pass

Sample secondary discipline plan

◣ Send your discipline plan home.

Include a sign-off portion that is to be returned to you, indicating that the parent has read the discipline plan.

Classroom Discipline Plan

Room 6   Mr. Brown

Dear Parent(s):

These are the rules of my classroom. These rules will be in effect at all times:

- Follow directions.
- Keep hands, feet, objects to yourself.
- No teasing or name calling.
- Do not leave the room without permission.

If a student chooses to break a rule, the following consequences will be imposed:

First time a student breaks a rule:	Warning
Second time:	Last in line for lunch
Third time:	Time-out area
Fourth time:	Teacher calls parents
Fifth time:	Send to principal

Severe misbehavior, such as fighting, verbal abuse will result in the immediate imposition of the Severe Clause: Send to principal.

Sample discipline plan letter

(continues)

Students who behave appropriately will be positively rewarded with praise, positive notes sent home, small rewards, class parties, and other special privileges.

I have already discussed this plan with your child, but I would appreciate it if you would review it together, then sign and return the form below.

Thank you for your support.
Sincerely,

Mr. Brown

– –

I have read the discipline plan and have discussed it with my child.

Parent's signature_____

Student's signature_____

Date _____

Having well-defined rules and predetermined consequences from the very beginning will assist you in your teaching efforts and give you a basis for effectively communicating with parents. You will be able to:

• Judge student behavior fairly.

• Discuss behavior problems more confidently with parents.

Your reasons for calling a parent will never be vague or arbitrary. You can accurately describe to a parent:

• The rule(s) that the student has broken.

• The consequences of the student's misbehavior.

Your Homework Policy

Because homework is a day-to-day connection between home and school it is one of the best opportunities you have for positive interaction with parents. Homework has the potential to be a powerful part of your parent involvement program. Too often, however, homework becomes a bone of contention between parents, students and teachers. Any positive interaction that might result from it is lost in a sea of misinformation and unfulfilled expectations.

Homework has the potential to be a powerful part of your parent involvement program.

If you want parents to give the support you need regarding homework, it is important that your homework standards are clearly spelled out. You need to develop a homework policy. A homework policy clearly states your expectations for everyone involved in the homework process: student, teacher and parents.

A homework policy should:

1. Explain why homework is assigned.

2. Explain the types of homework you will assign.

3. Inform parents of the amount and frequency of homework.

4. Provide guidelines for when and how students are to complete homework.

5. State that you will keep a record of assignments completed and not completed.

6. Explain how homework will affect students' grades.

7. Inform parents and students of test schedules.

8. Let parents know how you will positively reinforce students who complete homework.

9. Explain what you will do when students do not complete homework (the affect on grades, etc.).

10. Clarify what is expected of the parent.

Let's look more closely at each of the elements of a homework policy:

1. Explain why homework is assigned.
You can't assume that parents understand why homework is given or how important it is. Therefore, you must explain the benefits of homework and why you are going to give it. For instance, your rationale could include that homework is important because:

• It reinforces skills and material learned in class.

• It prepares students for upcoming class topics.

• It teaches students to work independently.

• It aids in evaluating student progress.

• It teaches students to assume responsibility for their own work.

• It teaches students organizational and time-management skills.

2. Explain the types of homework you will assign.

It is important that both parents and students know that you are doing your part to ensure that students have the ability to do the homework you assign. Your policy should state that homework you assign will require only those skills students have already learned in class.

3. Inform parents of the amount and frequency of homework.

If parents are to back up your homework program, they must know when to expect assignments. Research has shown that regular homework assignments produce more learning than less consistently assigned homework. It is important, therefore, for you to include in your homework policy:

1. The days of the week on which you will assign homework.

2. The amount of time it should take students to complete homework.

The amount of homework you assign will depend on your community, your district, your principal, your class and even the individual student.

4. Provide guidelines for when and how students are to complete homework.

For students to meet your expectations about completing homework, you must clearly explain how you expect them to do their assignments. Typical expectations include:

• All assignments will be completed.

• Students will do homework on their own and to the best of their ability.

• Students will turn in work that is neatly done.

• Students will turn in homework on time.

• Students are responsible for making up homework assignments missed due to absence.

5. State that you will keep a record of assignments completed and not completed.

Your policy should state that you will keep a daily record of all homework assignments completed and not completed. The fact that you will check all homework is enough to motivate many students to do their homework. Also, this type of record keeping says something to both students and parents about the value you place on each and every assignment.

6. Explain how homework will affect students' grades.

Students and parents alike need to know if homework will be graded separately or as a percentage of another grade. Many schools list homework as a separate item on report cards. Others consider homework as part of a citizenship grade or a subject grade. Whatever system you or your school uses should be stated in your homework policy.

7. Inform parents and students of test schedules.

It is important that parents and students (especially in upper grades) know when tests will be scheduled and how they will be evaluated. The following is an example of a homework policy statement regarding tests for a math class.

> "Tests will be given periodically, usually on a Wednesday or a Friday. Adequate notice will be given for all tests. To prepare for tests, go over notes and corrected homework assignments. Any test that receives a D or an F must be returned within two days signed by a parent. There will be no makeup of low quiz or test scores."

8. Let parents know how you will positively reinforce students who complete homework.

Research has shown that positive reinforcement is useful in motivating students to do homework. Your policy, therefore, should include:

- Positive rewards for individual students: praise, awards, notes home to the parents.

- Positive rewards that can be earned by the entire class.

9. Explain what you will do when students do not complete homework.

It is important that students and parents clearly understand the consequences of not doing homework. Examples of actions that can be taken include the following:

• Have parents sign completed homework every night.

• Have elementary students miss recess to complete homework.

• Have secondary students eat lunch in detention room to complete homework.

• Have students complete homework in after-school detention.

• Lower students' grades.

Whatever consequences you choose must be clearly spelled out in your homework policy.

NOTE: Homework missed for legitimate reasons must be explained in a signed note from the parents.

10. Clarify what is expected of the parent.

Since you do not follow the homework and the students home, it is up to parents to see that homework is completed. Your homework policy needs to cover the specific type of support you expect from parents. You should expect parents to:

• Establish homework as a top priority for their children.

• Make sure that their children do homework in a quiet environment.

• Establish a daily homework time.

• Provide positive support when homework is completed.

• Not allow their children to get out of doing homework.

• Contact you if children have problems with homework.

◣ Send your homework policy home.

Parents need to receive your homework policy before the first homework assignments are given. Take a look at the sample homework policy letters to parents on pages 57-63. Notice that each of the elements previously listed is included in the letters.

Room 6 Homework Policy

To the family of _____ ,

Why I assign homework:

I believe homework is important because it is a valuable aid in helping students make the most of their experience in school. I give homework because it is useful in reinforcing what has been learned in class, prepares students for upcoming lessons, teaches responsibility and helps students develop positive study habits.

When homework will be assigned:

Homework will be assigned Monday through Thursday nights. Assignments should take students no more than one hour to complete each night, not including studying for tests and working on projects. Spelling tests will be given each Friday. I will give students at least one week's notice to study for all tests, and one written report will be assigned each grading period.

Student's homework responsibilities:

I expect students to do their best job on their homework. I expect homework to be neat, not sloppy. I expect students to do the work on their own and only ask for help after they have given it their best effort. I expect that all assignments will be turned in on time.

Sample homework policy for a fourth-grade class

(continues)

Teacher's homework responsibilities:

I will check all homework. Because I strongly believe in the value positive support plays in motivating children to develop good study habits, I will give students praise and other incentives when they do their homework.

Parent's homework responsibilities:

Parents are the key to making homework a positive experience for their children. Therefore, I ask that parents make homework a top priority, provide necessary supplies and a quiet homework environment, set a daily homework time, provide praise and support, not let children avoid homework, and contact me if they notice a problem.

If students do not complete homework:

If students choose not to do their homework, I will ask that parents begin checking and signing completed homework each night. If students still choose not to complete their homework, they also choose to lose certain privileges. If students choose to make up homework the next day, their homework will be accepted but they will receive a one-grade reduction on that assignment. If they choose not to make up missed assignments, students will receive a grade of F for the assignment missed and a 15-minute detention. The first time a student receives a detention for missed homework, I will contact the parents.

(continues)

If there is a legitimate reason why a student is not able to finish homework, please send a note to me on the day the homework is due stating the reason it was not completed. The note must be signed by the parent.

Please read and discuss this homework policy with your child. Then sign and return the bottom portion of this letter to school.

Mrs. Kerns

— — — — — — — — — — — — — — — — — — —

I have read this homework policy and have discussed it with my child.

Parent's signature _____

Student's signature _____

Date _____

Homework Policy

Mr. Walsh   9th Grade Social Studies

To the family of _____ ,

Why I assign homework:

I believe homework is important because it is a valuable aid in helping students make the most of their experience in school. I give homework because it reinforces what has been taught in class, prepares students for upcoming lessons and helps students develop self-discipline, responsibility and organizational skills.

When homework will be assigned:

Homework will be assigned Monday, Tuesday and Thursday nights, and should take students no more than one hour to complete (not including long-range projects and studying for tests). Most homework assignments will involve reading chapters in the textbook, answering study questions and completing related worksheets.

Tests:

Tests will be given periodically, usually on a Wednesday or a Friday. Adequate notice will be given for all tests. Any test that receives a D or an F must be returned within

Sample homework policy for a ninth-grade social studies class.

(continues)

two days signed by a parent. There will be no makeup of low quiz or test scores. Students will have at least a two-week's notice to study for tests, and one written report will be assigned each grading period.

Student's homework responsibilities:

- All assignments will be completed.
- Students are responsible for making up homework missed due to absence.
- Homework will be turned in on time.
- Students will turn in work that is neatly done.

If students choose not to do their homework, the following consequences may occur:

- Parents will be asked to sign completed homework each night.
- Students may be required to complete homework in the detention room during lunch.
- Students may be required to complete homework in after-school detention.

NOTE: If a student has four or more "no credit" homework assignments in any one quarter, it will result in the final grade being dropped a full letter grade.

(continues)

If there is a legitimate reason why a student is unable to finish homework, please send a note on the day the homework is due stating the reason it was not completed. The note must be signed by the parent.

Parent's homework responsibilities:

Parents are the key to making homework a positive experience for their children. Therefore, I ask that you make homework a top priority, provide necessary supplies and a quiet homework environment, provide praise and support and contact me if you notice a problem.

Teacher's homework responsibilities:

I will check all homework and keep a record of assignments completed and not completed. Because I strongly believe in the value positive support plays in motivating students to develop good study habits, I will give students praise and other incentives when they do their homework.

I am looking forward to enjoying an exciting, productive year at school. Please do not hesitate to call me if you have any questions regarding this homework policy or any other matter.

(continues)

Please read and discuss this homework policy with your child. Then sign and return the bottom portion of this letter to school.

Sincerely,

Mr. Jefferson

— — — — — — — — — — — — — — — — — — —

I have read this homework policy and have discussed it with my child.

Parent's signature _____

Student's signature _____

Date _____

⌐ It's worth the effort.

Take a moment to look back at the first-day goals in terms of moving parents past their roadblocks. How do you think parents will react to receiving these notes, letters and phone calls?

• The overwhelmed parent will be relieved and pleased that his or her child has a teacher who is taking charge and who obviously cares about the student. This parent will appreciate the confidence the teacher has shown in taking a pro-active stance.

• For the parent who wants to help but doesn't know how, the ice has been broken and an introduction made. He or she will feel much more comfortable now about reaching out to either ask for or accept help.

• Finally, the parent who has negative feelings towards school or teacher will most likely have been nudged just a little bit closer to a more positive attitude about both.

It may seem time-consuming to prepare these different parent communications, but keep in mind that you are setting the stage for a full year of positive parent involvement. By meeting each of these objectives, you are demonstrating your commitment to that involvement. Putting in time and energy early will save you even greater effort in the future. These are preventative actions that can put your parent involvement program on the right track—right from the start.

First-Day Objectives Do's and Don'ts

Do

- Initiate parent contact before the first day of school.

- Formulate your classroom discipline plan before school starts.

- Write your homework policy before school starts

- Send parents a letter telling them that you need their support, and that the education of their children is a team effort

- Contact parents of potential problem students to let them know you are committed to their children's success in school this year

- Send your discipline plan and homework policy home as soon as school begins. Ask parents to read and sign both documents.

- Carefully explain your discipline plan and homework policy to students on the first day of school

- Feel confident in your ability to have a successful year!

Don't

- Don't avoid contacting, by phone or by letter, non-English speaking parents. Find a translator to help you and reach out to these parents.

- Don't wait for parents to come to you. Reach out to them first— before school starts.

☑ First-Day Objectives Checklist

Refer to this checklist when you start your first-day objectives.

Have you:

____ Sent welcome notes to parents and students before school begins?

____ Sent home a letter of introduction?

____ Contacted parents of problem students before school begins?

____ Sent home a copy of your classroom discipline plan?

____ Sent home a copy of your homework policy?

Chapter **5**

Back-to-School Night

> **❝** *I work to get as many parents as possible to attend. The result: parent involvement success all year long!* **❞**

Back-to-School Night can be the most important event of the school year for both elementary and secondary teachers. It's your opportunity to meet parents, explain your policies and programs in detail, answer any questions about your class, and, most important, assure parents of your commitment to their children. The professionalism and confidence you project at Back-to-School Night can be instrumental toward getting parents on your side. Back-to-School Night can be a solitary event, unrelated to the rest of the year, or it can be the beginning of a dynamic year in which you and parents team up to become partners in their children's education. It all depends upon how you plan and deliver.

Unfortunately, we know that more than half of all parents don't attend Back-to-School Night. You may find that the very parents you want and need most to show up are the ones who don't. Don't just accept this; take action! Make a commitment to do all you can to encourage full parent participation. Use a variety of techniques to motivate parents to attend.

Here are some ideas that will help you plan and implement a great event:

• Send Back-to-School Night invitations.

• Involve students in planning.

• Use parent motivators to boost attendance.

• Plan your classroom environment.

• Know exactly what you will say to parents.

• Present special Back-to-School Night activities.

◤ Send invitations.

Make sure parents receive personalized invitations from you. Let them know that you are really counting on their attendance, and that Back-to-School Night is an important responsibility for both of you. Use the invitation to publicize some of the events planned and, most important, list compelling reasons why parents should attend. Include a tear-off RSVP portion that will encourage parents to commit to attending. Be sure to send this invitation well in advance so parents can make plans. Send a follow-up reminder a few days before.

To:_____

You're Invited to **Back-to-School Night!**

Place_____

Date_____

Time_____

- See what we're doing in class.
- Learn what you can do at home to help your child be successful in school!
- Participate in the Back-to-School Night raffle! Prizes!
- Enjoy a video presentation starring your child!
- Take home a **FREE** Parent Handbook filled with great ideas for you and your child.

Please join us.

Working Together We Can Make a Difference!

Babysitting will be available in Room 6.
- -

☐ I will be attending Back-to-School Night.

☐ I won't be able to attend Back-to-School Night.

Name_____

Parent of _____

*Sample
Back-to-School
Night
invitation*

NOTE: Many parents cannot get away at night because they do not have a babysitter. Set up a schoolwide babysitting service for Back-to-School Night and you will see better attendance. Make sure that all parents are informed of the service.

Involve students in planning.

Students at any grade level can help you create an inviting classroom atmosphere by designing "Welcome Parents" signs and other classroom posters or displays for Back-to-School Night. In addition, try to involve students in preparing some of your Back-to-School Night activities or presentations (see pages 80-81 for suggestions). By doing so, you will generate enthusiasm that they can pass on to parents.

Boost parent attendance.

Your first Back-to-School Night objective is to get parents there. To boost parent attendance, you may have to offer a few incentives. Try some of these ideas:

Hold a Back-to-School Night raffle.
Attending parents get to place signed raffle tickets in a jar. During a subsequent school day, the teacher pulls out several raffle tickets and gives prizes to the winning students. School supplies (markers, pocket dictionary, compass) make excellent prizes. Inform parents of the raffle ahead of time. And be sure to tell students, too, so they can help motivate their parents to participate.

Play Back-to-School Night lotto.
Each parent who attends Back-To-School Night writes his or her name in a space on a special Back-to-School Night lotto board. Later, in school, the teacher pulls the winning numbers and awards prizes to students whose parents' names were drawn.

Give Back-to-School Night bonus tickets.
Any student whose parent(s) attends Back-to-School Night receives a ticket entitling the student to a special privilege or award, such as free reading time, a pencil or a notepad.

Dear Parent(s)

We missed you at Back-to-School Night.

I am sending you the Parent Handbook that I distributed at Back-to-School Night. It's filled with lots of information that will be useful as the year goes on. Please call me if you have any questions at all about anything in the handbook.

At Back-to-School Night, all of the parents filled out raffle tickets for a classroom drawing. We will be having this drawing in a couple of days and students will win prizes such as pencils, rulers and other school supplies. To make sure your child participates in the raffle, please fill out the coupon on the bottom of this letter and send it back to school as soon as possible.

....

Back-to-School Night Raffle.
Working together we can make a difference!

Parent's name_____

Student's name_____

Sample letter to parents who did not attend

For parents who can't attend: Some parents simply cannot come to Back-to-School Night. Others just don't. Regardless of the reason, you owe it to yourself and your students to make another effort to contact them with your Back-to-School Night message.

Avoid penalizing a student whose parent didn't attend.

Reach out to those parents who weren't there. The next day send home any materials you distributed at Back-to-School Night along with a note inviting the parent to take part in the raffle, or other incentive you used. (By doing so, you will avoid penalizing a student whose parent didn't attend.) Remember, you don't want to disenfranchise any parent. You want them all solidly behind you. Your willingness to go the extra mile will further demonstrate your commitment to all of your students.

`abc` Plan the classroom environment.

First impressions really count at Back-to-School Night, so make a point of creating an environment that is inviting, friendly and projects the mood you want parents to feel: involved and welcomed. Let the room speak for you. Set the mood by hanging a bright "Welcome Parents" poster in the front of the room.

Here are other items that should be displayed:

• Class schedule (on board)

• Displays of work completed and curriculum in progress

• Centers or areas labeled clearly

Get to know each other . . .
Introducing yourself to parents will be easier if everyone is wearing a name tag. Put a supply of adhesive-backed tags near the classroom door and ask parents to write their names as they enter. You may wish to prepare name tags that leave a space for the student's name also. This will help you identify parents who may have a different last name than the student. Name tags will help parents get acquainted with each other, too.

Know what you will say.

Be prepared. Know what you are going to say, when you are going to say it, and how you expect parents to participate. Back-to-School Night should be carefully orchestrated so that all of your goals will be met. Make sure you prepare an outline of the topics you will be talking about to parents. This is no time to get nervous and leave out important information. It's perfectly ok (and a smart idea) to refer to note cards as you speak.

Your Back-to-School Night goal should be to convince parents of two things:

- Parents are the most important people in a child's life. As such, parents are in a unique position to help children achieve their highest potential.

- You sincerely care about their children and are committed to seeing them succeed.

Everything you say or do should be geared to achieving these goals. You began by sending out thoughtful, personal invitations. Now continue by carefully planning what you will say. Here is a Back-to-School Night script you may wish to use as a guide. Your words will of course differ, but all of these major points should be included in your own presentation. If any of your student's parents are non-English speaking, make sure you have a translator available. Remember, even when using a translator, to look directly at parents as you speak. Smile, make eye contact and project the confidence you want the parents to feel.

What to Say to Parents
Emphasize to parents that they are the most important people in their child's life.

 I'd like to start tonight by giving you all a little quiz. Don't panic! It's short and you didn't need to prepare. In fact, there's only one question: Which of the following is the key to a child's success in school? A. The competence of the teacher. B. The competence of the principal C. The motivation and support of parents.

"The answer is C. You—the parents—are the key to your

child's success. Over and over again, research has proved that the best schools, the best teachers, the best principals are not as important to a child's achievement in school as a parent is. You have more ability to motivate, more ability to stimulate, more ability to get your child to succeed than anyone, or anything else.

Because you are so important, it is my job to do everything in my power to work with you. My responsibility as a teacher is to educate your children. I need your support and backing."

Explain when and how you will communicate with parents.

 Because you are so important to your child's success, it's my responsibility to stay in touch with you and let you know how your child is doing-and what we can do to work together.

"First, when your child does well in school, I think you need to know about it. I'm sure many of you have had the experience of being contacted by school only when there's a problem. Well, I feel it is even more important for you to hear from me when your child is doing something right! Some of you have already heard from me in this respect. And it felt good, didn't it?

"On the other hand, if your child is not doing as well as he or she should be, I will let you know. I feel that you as a parent have the right to know how your child is doing, and if there are any problems. I'm a parent myself. I have children and I want to know how they are doing in school. I have a right to know, just as you do. Thus, any time I feel your child's behavior is such that you need to be informed, you will hear from me. I will not wait until the problem gets out of hand. I will not wait until parent conference time. I will call you as soon as I feel you need to know what's going on."

Describe your classroom discipline plan.

To further clarify how we will work together, I have established a fair, consistent, positive plan for dealing with students' behavior in class. All of you have received a copy of my classroom discipline plan. You have all read the rules of the classroom, the consequences students will receive if they choose to break the rules, and—most important—the fact that I will positively motivate students to follow these rules.

"You probably noticed that the plan states that under certain conditions I will contact parents. You can be assured, however, that before I contact you I will have already taken steps to help your child. In addition, I would like to make it very clear that I believe the key to dealing with students is to support and praise them when they make good choices."

Describe your homework policy.

I'm aware that homework has probably been the cause of more than one evening battle in your home. You've probably wished sometimes that homework would just disappear. I'm sure your kids feel that way! But I want you to understand that I give homework for some very important reasons. Homework teaches a child responsibility and good study habits. These are skills that they must develop if they are to succeed in school and, in the future, at work. Homework also increases a student's knowledge of a subject area. Believe me, I know that homework demands a lot from all of us. Because of that, I don't give homework assignments that are meaningless. You can be assured that every homework assignment I give is designed to meet specific educational objectives.

"All of you have received a copy of my homework policy. This homework policy explains how I will deal with homework in my class this year. Your children know exactly what to expect regarding homework. They know that I will give them positive reinforcement when they do their homework according to the guidelines in the homework policy. On the other hand, they will choose to accept consequences if they do not do their homework. The homework policy also states that if your child has problems with homework that can't be worked out at school, I will contact you so we can work together to help him or her.

Tell parents what you need from them.

" I've told you what I plan to do to help your child have a successful, happy year. Now I need to share with you some of the things your child needs from you and what I need from you to ensure that successful year. You're here tonight. That's a great start. I also need your support all year long. Here's what I mean.

"First, I need you to back my academic efforts. I need you to send your children a very clear message: 'I expect you to do your very best work. I expect you to work to your full potential.' You have to let your children know that their education is important to you.

"Second, I need you to communicate to your children that you expect them to behave and follow the rules of the classroom. They must know that you will not tolerate them misbehaving in class or anywhere else at school. They must know that if they misbehave, and I have to contact you, that you will follow up at home by providing additional consequences. Your child must understand that you will back me 100%.

"Third, you must also make sure that your children do their homework. What exactly does this mean?

1. You must let your children know that homework is a top priority at home.
2. You must make sure your children have a quiet place in which to do homework.
3. You should decide upon a predetermined time when

your child will do homework each night. And you should insist that homework be done during this time.

4. You must give positive support when your child does do homework, and provide consequences when they choose not to. It is vital that your children know you are serious about them doing homework.

"Finally, I need your commitment to contact me whenever you feel there is something we should discuss. If you have any concerns whatsoever, pick up the phone and call. Believe me, I want to hear from you. If your child is unhappy, complains, or is upset about something, pick up the phone and call. If there are changes in your family, a problem or crisis that is effecting your child, let me know. If your child is having problems with homework don't try to do it for him. Pick up the phone and call. You're not bothering me. Your child's welfare is my concern, too. Remember, I can't do the best job for him or her unless I'm kept informed."

Convey your confidence.

 I have complete confidence that if we work together your children can have a great year. But I can't do it on my own. I'll do my best for your children, every day. Just remember, you are the real key to your child's success. Your influence with your child is more powerful than anyone else's. That's why I want you on my side. I want your children to succeed this year. Together, we're going to see that happen. It's going to be a great year! I'm looking forward to working with each and every one of you."

As you speak, be sure to pause occasionally and ask parents if they have any questions. Take notes on what is asked, or about any other issues that may arise. You can respond to any concerns in a Back-to-School Night follow-up letter (see page 82). It's important to let parents know that they are being listened to.

◆ Other discussion points:

Here are some other points you may want to include in your presentation:

Give parents suggestions for how they can help at home.
Remember, parents often don't help their children with schoolwork because they just don't know what to do or how to go about doing it. Be prepared to give parents some specific ideas for helping their children at home. If, for example, students are beginning to print, send home a manuscript letter practice sheet. If students are learning multiplication facts, send home copies of flash cards that can be cut out. If students will soon be tackling a term paper, give the parents guidelines for helping with that project. Be sure to explain to parents how these materials are to be used. Follow up throughout the year with "helping at home" updates as the curriculum changes.

Introduce parents to Power Reading.
Reading comprehension skills are the basis for success in all subject areas. Parents can help their children develop these skills at home with the Power Reading technique. Here's how to introduce it:

To do well in all subjects at school, students must have strong reading comprehension skills. This means that they understand what they are reading. You can help your child develop these skills with a technique called Power Reading. Here's how it works:

"First, read aloud to your child for five minutes. Be sure that the book from which you are reading is at your child's reading level. Pronounce words carefully and clearly, and make appropriate pauses for periods and commas.

"Next, listen to your child read. Have your child continue reading the same book aloud for another five minutes. He or she should begin at the point where you stopped reading. Remind your child to take it slowly and read so that the words makes sense. This is why your oral reading is so important. It's setting an example for your child. Don't stop and correct your child while he or she is reading.

"Finally, ask questions about what was read. Check how well your child was listening and reading by asking general questions about the material you read aloud and the material he or she read aloud. Talk about the story together.

"I suggest that you hold a Power Reading session with your child as often as possible. It's an excellent way to improve reading skills and demonstrate the importance you place on reading. Start a book that's of particular interest to your child and continue using the same book for Power Reading sessions until it's completed. I'd be glad to give you some suggestions for books that are appropriate for your child."

Send a Power Reading sheet home with parents.
We have included a Power Reading tip sheet on Appendix pages 239-240. Give this to parents at Back-to-School Night.

Invite parents to help at school.
Volunteers can be a great help to you in your classroom. Do some recruiting at Back-to-School Night! Think ahead of time about the kind of help you'd like to receive from parents. Then put together a volunteer request letter. Make sure you offer some creative alternatives for working parents who can't be in the classroom during the school day (they like to help, too). Ideas might include creating posters for the classroom or helping out on a Saturday classroom improvement project. And don't hesitate to ask parents what they'd like to do. You just might have a talented storyteller, musician, puppeteer, scientist or chef among your parents.

Don't hesitate to ask for volunteers.

⭐ Present special activities.

You've encouraged parents to attend, created an inviting atmosphere and spoken to them with assurance and clarity. Don't stop now! There are other activities that you can incorporate into Back-to-School Night that will round out the evening and help make a lasting impression. Here are some entertaining suggestions that can make the event an even greater success.

Take parents on a tour of the classroom.

Parents are interested in what their children are learning at school so take this opportunity to show off your classroom! Don't assume that parents understand the reasons behind your classroom organization and materials. Explain everything. Let them know why you have a listening center filled with a jumble of headsets (for individualized instruction). Explain the reason for the hamster cage (to teach responsibility). Point out your classroom library with pride and tell the parents how it will be used. Explain to parents that the classroom and its contents will be the students' learning laboratory for a year. Get the parents excited about it. Your educational plans will come alive for parents if they are given the opportunity feel a part of them. Encourage parents to ask questions about anything they see.

Explain everything you have in your classroom.

Give parents a "private screening."

All parents love to see their children (whatever their age) in a starring role. Present a slide or video presentation showing students in their daily classroom routines—entering the classroom, working in small groups, doing independent seatwork, moving to centers, etc. Don't forget a group shot of the entire class. Make sure every student appears in the slide show.

Make tape recordings.

Play a tape recording of students discussing classroom activities.

Have elementary students tape record a song to be played for parents. Then at Back-to-School Night have parents sing and record a song to be played for students the next day.

Have students write notes to parents.
Have each student leave a note written to his or her parent. The note is left in the student's desk. (In upper grades the notes could be kept in a class folder and distributed to parents.) At Back-to-School Night the parents read the notes and write a return message to their child. In elementary grades these notes can be left for students on their own desks.

Create and distribute a Parent Handbook.
Hand out a packet of information that parents can take home with them. This Parent Handbook is a convenient way to give parents a lot of information in one package. Here is a list of items you might want to include:

• Class list (It's especially helpful for parents of primary children to know the names of their child's classmates.)

• Staff list, school address, phone number, school hours

• Map of the school

• Schoolwide rules

• Discipline plan (if not sent in a separate letter)

• Daily classroom schedule

• Grade level curriculum

• Manuscript or cursive writing guide

• School/calendar year showing all school holidays and non-teaching days

• Blank teacher/parent communication forms

• Policies about absences, medical appointments, making up classwork

• Tips on how to help a child study at home

• Suggested reading lists

• Health concerns (nutrition, exercise, sleep)

Write the name of each student on a Parent Handbook. After Back-to-School Night send the ones that are not picked up home to parents (see page 71).

⬕ Keep the spirit alive!

Don't let the enthusiasm generated by Back-to-School Night just fade away. Use it to your advantage! Let parents know how much you appreciated their participation. A few days afterward, send a brief note home thanking parents for attending. Update them on any items that might have come under discussion at Back-to-School Night. And, because it's sometimes difficult for parents to speak up and air their concerns in front of a whole group, you might also include a "return message" section where parents can write back to you with any questions they may have. This follow-up note is also an excellent way to make contact with parents who did not attend Back-to-School Night.

Let parents know how much you appreciated their participation.

The sense of teamwork, camaraderie and excitement you cultivate at Back-to-School Night is a great way to help parents overcome the roadblocks that keep them from giving you support. By doing so, you will also increase your own confidence in just how successful you can be in getting parents on your side.

Back-to-School Night Do's and Don'ts

Do

- Speak to every parent. Call them by name and refer to their child by name (name tags can help make this easier).
- Plan what you will say. Keep your notes with you as you speak.
- Provide a program that allows each student to be highlighted in some way (through photographs, tape recordings, video, classwork, artwork).
- Focus on the responsibility of parent and teacher to work as partners in children's education.
- Provide relevant, informative material for parents to take home.
- Encourage parents to offer their own special talents and interests to the classroom as the year goes on.
- Plan your Back-to-School Night schedule as thoroughly as you would a day in class.
- Have translators available if necessary.
- Listen to parents. Take notes about any questions or concerns that are brought up. Follow up on these concerns.
- Reach out to parents who didn't attend. Send all Back-to-School Night materials home the next day.
- Send out a Back-to-School Night follow-up letter.

Don't

- Don't expect parents to come just because the school sent home a notice. Reach out! It's up to you to get the parents of your students there.
- Don't talk only about curriculum. Remember, your first goal should be to convince parents of the important role they play in their children's education.
- Don't talk down to parents or be intimidated by them. Approach them as equals, but keep in mind that you are the professional educator.
- Don't make the mistake of thinking that exciting Back-to-School Nights are for elementary classes only. Parents of older students also appreciate a motivating presentation.

☑ Back-to-School Night Checklist

Refer to this checklist as you plan your Back-to-School Night.

Have you:

____ Sent home invitations to parents that explain why Back-to-School Night is so important?

____ Planned to use a "parent motivator" to help get parents to attend?

____ Written down what you want to say to parents?

____ Created a welcoming environment in your classroom?

____ Created a Parent Handbook to give to parents at Back-to-School Night?

____ Decided on the activities you will present?

____ Arranged for a translator if necessary?

____ Decided to send a Back-to-School Night follow-up letter to parents?

Positive Communication with Parents

Chapter **6**

66 *. . .just pick up the phone and say something nice. It's like giving a gift.* 99

Show you care! For effective teachers these are really words to live by. Every day, all year long, using positive communication is imperative for showing that you care and for getting past the roadblocks that keep parents from giving support. Parents view educators who consistently communicate positive news to them as educators who are truly concerned about their children. And the more a parent feels you are concerned, the more he or she will listen and support you. Unless you are prepared to pursue consistent

85

positive communication with parents, you will have a difficult time getting all the parents on your side. In this chapter we will look at some proven techniques teachers use to positively communicate with parents.

Here's what we'll cover:

• Positive phone calls

• Notes, cards and letters

• Home visits

• Parent communication activities

Positive communication won't happen if you don't schedule it!

A note to middle school and secondary teachers: Don't let the large number of students you teach deter you from making positive contact with parents. In upper grades the best way to reach all parents is through a schoolwide plan in which teachers are organized so that all parents receive regular, planned positive contact.

You can still, however, reach out to parents regularly even if you're on your own. Planning is the answer. You'd be surprised at the number of students you can reach if you just schedule time for positives. A quick positive phone call, for example, is easy to make and takes only a couple of minutes (see page 87). Make two brief calls each afternoon and you've reached ten parents a week. Multiply that by 36 weeks and you've reached 360 parents. As you read about the positive communication techniques in this chapter, give thought to how you could schedule them into your week. Then set a goal of reaching a specific number of parents each week.

Two calls each day equals 360 calls a year!

Above all, keep this in mind: it won't happen if you don't schedule it.

Positive Phone Calls

One of the most effective parent communication techniques at your disposal is a quick phone call home to let parents know how well their child is doing. It doesn't have to be a long conversation—just a brief update and a few friendly words. Get into the habit of phoning parents with good news and it won't be so difficult to call them when there is a problem to be solved. You'll have already established a comfortable relationship, and parents will be much more likely to listen to what you have to say.

Here are the points you'll want to cover in a positive phone call:

Describe the student's positive behavior.
Start off the call by telling the parent the specific positive behavior the student exhibited in your classroom.

> *"Chris is off to a great start this semester. He's completed all his class assignments and homework this week."*

Describe how you feel about the student's positive behavior.
Let the parent know how pleased you are with the student's good behavior or academic performance. Remember, this may be the first time the parent has heard anything positive about his or her child in a long time!

> *"I'm very pleased that Doug is showing such improvement in math this year. His hard work is getting results."*

Ask the parent to share the content of the conversation with the student.
Your conversation with the parent will have an even greater impact if the parent tells the child about the call. It is important that the student knows that both you and the parent are proud of his or her accomplishments.

> *"Please tell Roberto that I called and how pleased I am with his behavior in class."*

"When Lisa gets home please share our conversation with her. I think it will be great for her to know that I called and how pleased we both are with her performance in school."

Here's a sample positive phone conversation:

Teacher: Mrs. Suarez, this is Mrs. Endicott, Jose's math teacher. I just wanted to let you know how well Jose is doing in school. He is a really hard worker. He gets right to work on all of his assignments, follows directions beautifully, and always seems to do the best job he can.

Parent: Well, he does seem to be liking school more this year.

Teacher: I'm glad to hear that. I really enjoy having him in my classroom.

Parent: I appreciate your telling me this. It's really made my day!

Teacher: Well, I believe it's just as important to tell parents when their child is doing well in school as it is when they're having problems.

Parent: That makes sense to me.

Teacher: It makes sense to me, too. There's one last thing. Please let Jose know that I called and how happy I am about how well he's doing in class. I want to be sure he knows that his good work is noticed by all of us.

Parent: I sure will! Thank you!

Notes, Cards and Letters

The school year will be filled with occasions that call for positive parent communication. Take advantage of as many of these "good news opportunities" as possible.

Positive Notes to Parents

An effective way to give parents positive feedback on their child's performance in school is through positive notes. A positive note is simply a few lines written to a parent that tells something good about their child. Once you get into the habit of sending home a predetermined number of notes each week, it will become a natural part of your routine. And this habit will pay dividends. Imagine how much easier it will be to contact a parent about a problem if they've already heard from you in a positive context!

• Keep a file of ready-to-use positive notes and preaddressed envelopes in your desk.

• Plan to send home a specific number of notes each week.

• When writing notes, address the parents by name and mention the student's name, too. Keep the notes brief and to the point:

October 14

Dear Mr. and Mrs. Brown,

Just wanted to let you know what a terrific job Sara did today in giving her oral report to the class. Her presentation was both informative and entertaining. You should be proud of the good work she is doing!
Sincerely,

Mr. Smith

Sample positive note

Good Behavior Messages and Academic Awards

In addition to personalized notes, send home behavior messages or academic awards to parents. Many of these awards are commercially available with a preprinted message ("Thought you'd like to know that _____'s behavior in class today was terrific!"). All you have to do is add the child's name and send the award home with the student.

Sample good behavior message

The spotlight is on YOU for good behavior!

Birthday Greetings

To students: What better way to let parents know that you care about their child than sending home a birthday card. When it arrives in the mail, everyone in the family sees that you do care. If you have access to a computer and printer, you can easily run off cards that are personalized both with words and graphics. Keep a class birthday list in your plan book so you can be prepared.

To parents: Everybody likes a little special recognition on birthdays. Parents will be especially pleased that you've taken the time and interest to remember them.

Try this: Have students create a birthday card for each parent as an art project at the beginning of the year. File them away by date and send home when appropriate.

Get-Well Cards and Phone Calls

When students are sick, parents are worried, work schedules are upset and life becomes more complicated for families. This is a good opportunity to show your concern for your student and his or her parents. When a student is sick for more than a few days, send home a get-well card or pick up the phone and see how the child is doing. You can also use this opportunity to update the parent on the child's classwork.

Here's an example of a get-well phone call:

> Mrs. Lee? Hi. This is Sandra Hyatt, David's teacher. We've missed David this week and I just wanted to give you a call and see how he's doing. Everyone in the class sends their best wishes. We're looking forward to having him back.
>
> "I know he may be concerned about the work he's missing, but tell him to concentrate on getting well! I'll work with him on catching up when he's feeling better."

Thank-You Notes

Throughout the year parents will help you in many ways: donating supplies to the classroom, volunteering time, chaperoning field trips or dances, or helping their child with a project. Don't let these good deeds go unrecognized. Parents will be more motivated to help out again if they feel their contribution was appreciated. Keep a supply of thank-you notes on hand and use them often. Students too will notice and feel proud when these acknowledgments go home.

Each Friday spend a few minutes reviewing the week. Jot down the names of parents who made that special effort you appreciate and send home a note to each.

Don't let good deeds go unrecognized.

Home Visits

Nothing is quite as personal, or demonstrates your concern and caring, as a visit to a student's home. This is especially true when the purpose of a home visit is simply to say hello, meet the family and talk to the parent about the positive things the student is doing in school. A home visit can be a wonderful experience for student, parent and teacher. For the parent, it's an opportunity to meet the teacher in comfortable, familiar and relaxed surroundings. For the student, its a chance to clearly see that home and school are a team that's working together. For you, a home visit can give you a better perspective on a student's life away from school.

You will find that once you have met personally with parents under such positive circumstances, it will be all the easier to contact them about any problems that arise as the year proceeds.

• Try to make as many home visits as you can at the start of the year.

• Be sure to call the parent ahead of time to schedule a date and time for the visit. Don't just drop in!

Parent Communication Ideas

When parents are connected with what's going on in your classroom it will be easier for you to stay connected with them. Keep parents informed about schoolwork and other classroom activities.

Have students keep a daily "school-to-home" journal.
When parents ask their child, "What happened in school today?" the answer is often, "nothing." You can encourage better public relations than this! A daily journal that goes back and forth between home and school can keep parents and students communicating. At the end of each day have students write a few sentences telling what went on in school that day. Each night students take the journals home to be read by parents. Parents sign the day's entry and the student returns the journal to school.

Send student work home each Friday in a "Special Delivery to Parents" envelope.
The more a parent knows about a child's work at school, the higher the probability you will get the support you need. Plan to send a folder or large envelope home each Friday containing student work from the previous week. The folder should include space for the parents to sign, indicating that they looked at the child's work. You may also wish to include space for parents to make comments. Students should be instructed to return the folder to school on Monday. (Positive notes and awards can be sent home in the folders, too.)

Weekly Classroom Newsletter
Send a newsletter home each week informing parents about classroom activities and upcoming events. But don't do all of the work yourself! This method of communication will be even more effective if students help create it.

Here are two newsletter ideas:

For primary grades: **Weekly Family Letter**

Every Friday each student writes three or more sentences telling what he or she did during that week. The sentences are turned in and the teacher compiles them into one big letter (typed), making sure that a sentence from each child is included. The letter is addressed to "Dear Family." On Monday, the teacher gives each student a copy of the letter. The students underlines the sentence he or she wrote and takes the letter home to show to proud parents.

Suggestions for use:
Send a note home to parents with the first Weekly Family Letter. Make sure they understand that this letter will be a weekly group effort, and that their child's writing will be included each week. Suggest that they ask their child to read the whole letter to them each week and spend some time talking about the events recorded in the letter.

Keep all of the weekly letters in a three-ring binder. As the weeks go by, students will enjoy looking back at their classroom experiences. You may wish to occasionally add photographs to add further interest to this very lively history.

For upper grades: **Family Newsletter**

Older students will enjoy having a hand in planning and producing a weekly (or bi-weekly) newsletter. As a class project, decide on regular columns that will be included in the newsletter. Assign committees to be responsible for gathering the information for and writing each column. Rotate assignments throughout the year. Suggestions for columns:

A Message from the Teacher
We're Proud of These Students!
Upcoming Projects and Assignments
Special Events
Opinion Poll
What We Need (what parents can do specifically to help the class or school)

Family NewsLetter

A Message from the Teacher

Upcoming Projects and Assignments

We're Proud of These Students!

Special Events

Sample family newsletter format

⌐⌐ Stay on track by keeping track!

Because you want to be sure that all students and parents are receiving equal, positive attention, it's important to keep track of the notes and awards you send home. Set up a column in your roll book or plan book to record this information. List each student's name. When a note or award goes home, or a phone call is made, jot down the date on the line next to the name. Get into the habit of reviewing this list regularly.

It is most important that you send home positive notes to parents of students who are potential problems or who have been problems in the past. The more the parents of these children hear good news, the greater the probability of your getting their support when you need it. And the support of these parents is vital to their child's achievement as well as to a smooth-running classroom.

Positive Communication with Parents Do's and Don'ts

Do

• Make special effort to communicate positively with parents of students who have had problems in the past

• Set goals for sending home a specific number of positive notes each week.

• Make positive home visits at the start of the year, and all year long.

• Keep track of all parent communications.

• Phone parents with positive updates on academic and behavior successes.

• Keep the positive communication momentum going all year long.

Don't

• Don't underestimate how important positive notes and phone calls to parents are. They really do want to hear good news from you!

• Don't forget to give positive reinforcement to the students who always behave and do their work. They shouldn't be ignored.

• Don't forget to say thank you to parents any time they help you out.

• Don't make negative communication the first contact you have with parents.

☑ Positive Communication with Parents Checklist

Refer to this checklist as you plan Positive Communication with Parents.

Have you:

_____ Set goals for sending home positive notes to parents? How many notes will you plan to send home each week?

_____ Started making positive phone calls to parents? Once you try it, you'll like it. It's easy, effective and always welcomed!

_____ Made a birthday list of students and set aside birthday cards so you'll always be prepared?

_____ Put together a collection of get-well cards and thank-you notes for use throughout the year?

_____ Set up a record-keeping system to keep track of your positive communications?

_____ Planned to send home a classroom newsletter to keep parents informed about what's going on in your classroom?

Parents and Homework

Chapter **7**

66 *Homework is a great opportunity for getting parents involved in their child's educational experiences.* 99

Homework has the potential to be the most consistent day-to-day contact you can have with parents, particularly in the upper elementary grades and in secondary school. Yet parents complain that homework is often the greatest cause of conflict between them and their children. Likewise, teachers complain that students don't complete assignments and parents won't follow up to see that they do. The result? In most classrooms an important parent involvement resource goes to waste. Changing homework from an irritant into a positive is what we will deal with in this chapter.

The homework process has the potential to increase a student's self-esteem.

Too often, homework remains a mystery to parents. They don't understand why homework is given, when it will be given, how it is expected to be done, or what they can do to help. In short, parents' responsibilities in the homework process are usually never really addressed. All they know for sure about homework is that it's often a problem. This is unfortunate for both parent and student because the homework process also has the potential to increase a student's self-esteem. When parent and child work together, the child knows that he or she is important enough for the parent to stop, pay attention and get involved. And that's a good feeling for a child to have.

As mentioned in Chapter 4, teachers who are committed to involving parents in the homework process start by developing a homework policy. The policy establishes a firm foundation for homework by stating the expectations of everyone involved—students, parents and teacher. Your homework policy is just the beginning, though. You need to follow through all year long by keeping parents well informed about classwork, upcoming tests and projects, and ways in which they can help their children study more successfully. In this chapter we will take a look at four ways you can turn homework into a parent-involvement plus:

1. Help parents help their children do a better job on homework.

2. Keep the lines of communication open.

3. Assign Family Weekend Learning Activities

4. Help parents solve their children's most common homework problems.

▓ Help parents help their children do a better job on homework.

Many parents want to help their children do better with homework, but they don't know where to begin. Start the year off by providing parents with useful homework and study skills tips. (You will find complete reproducible sheets of these tips on pages 241-271 in the Appendix.) With these tips, parents can start immediately to improve their child's homework performance. Plan to send these sheets home at the beginning of the year.

Here's a summary of what's included:

Homework Tips

Good homework habits must be developed if a student is to do homework successfully. These five homework tips will guide parents in helping their children organize and complete homework each night.

Homework Tip #1:   Set up a study area.
Gives parents guidelines for helping their child choose a study area.
To do homework successfully, a student must have a place at home in which to work. The study area must be well-lit, quiet and have all necessary supplies close at hand.

Homework Tip #2:   Create a Homework Survival Kit.
Helps parents collect all the materials needed for homework.
Students can waste a lot of time in last-minute frenzied searches for homework supplies. This homework tip will help parents put together a Homework Survival Kit for their children that contains all the materials they will usually need to complete their homework assignments.

Homework Tip #3:   Schedule daily homework time.
Guides parents in helping their child choose a daily homework time.
Probably the touchiest homework issue students deal with is finding the time to do homework. Every parent knows that kids will find time for sports, TV and talking on the telephone, but somehow time runs

Motivate Your Child with Praise

Children need encouragement and support from the people whose opinions they value the most—their parents. Your consistent praise can increase your child's self-confidence and motivate him or her to do the best work possible.

Try these ideas:

• Each night praise your child about some specific accomplishment, for example, "I really like how you have been doing your homework as soon as we get home."

• Use **Super Praise** to motivate your child.

First, one parent praises the child: "I really appreciate how hard you're working to do your homework. You finished it all and you did such a nice job. Your printing is so neat and easy to read. I want to make sure Dad hears about this."

Second, this parent praises the child in front of the other parent: "Amanda did a wonderful job on her homework today. She started it without complaining, she stayed with it, and she did a super job on it."

Finally, the other person praises the child: "I feel so proud of you, getting such a good report from Mom. You're really doing fine!"

If you're a single parent, you can use a grandparent, a neighbor, or a family friend as your partner in delivering Super Praise. Any adult whose approval your child will value can fill the role of the second person offering praise.

Homework Tip Sheet #5 (Appendix page 246)

out when homework needs to be done. Parents can help their children schedule daily homework time, and get them to stick to it!

Homework Tip #4:   Encourage children to work independently.

Gives parents guidelines for encouraging children to work on their own. Homework teaches students responsibility. Through homework, students learn skills they must develop if they are to grow to be independent, successful adults. This homework tip gives parents "words of wisdom" about encouraging children to do their work on their own.

Homework Tip #5:   Motivate children with praise.

Gives parents techniques for motivating their children with praise. Because children need encouragement and support from the people whose opinions they value the most, praise is the best motivational tool parents can use. This homework tip will give parents suggestions for using praise to motivate their children.

Study Skills Tips

Knowing how to study is an important part of successful learning. But good study habits don't just happen. They must be taught in school and reinforced at home.

Give parents guidelines for helping their child in three key study areas: long-range planning, writing reports and studying for tests. Send these study skills tips home only if appropriate to the ages and needs of your students.

Study Skills Tip #1:   How to Help with Long-Range Planning

Assignments such as book reports, written reports and science projects are often overwhelming for students (and parents) because they require advance planning and time management. Because students usually don't know how to structure their time, the bulk of the work is often left to do at the last minute. Study Skills Tip #1 gives parents a long-range planner and guidelines for helping their child use it. A long-range planner can help students break a big assignment down into smaller tasks, each with its own deadline.

How to Help with Long-Range Planning

A Long-Range Planner can teach your child how to successfully complete longer projects. By using the Long-Range Planner, your child will learn how to break down a big project into small, easily completed tasks.

Using the Long-Range Planner

When your child brings home a long-range project, take time to help him or her determine the steps that have to be followed to complete the project. Once the assignment has been broken down into more easily managed steps, work together to establish the time period in which each step will be completed. Write the steps and the dates of completion on the Long-Range Planner. If each goal is met, there will be no last-minute panic before the report is due. See the example on this page of a completed Long-Range Planner for a term report.

> 1 Break down your BIG assignments into all of the smaller steps it takes to get the project done.
> 2 Write down your "mini" due dates for each step.
> 3 Fill in the final due date for the project on your last step.
>
> **LONG-RANGE PLANNER**
>
> Assignment Term report   Due Date 3/6
>
> 1 Pick out the topic of the report.   Due Date 2/2
> 2 Do fact-finding research   Due Date 2/11
> 3 Decide what questions I want to answer in report.   Due Date 2/15
> 4 Take notes about the topic.   Due Date 2/22
> 5 Write the rough draft.   Due Date 2/29
> 6 Write the final draft.   Due Date 3/6
> 7   Due Date

Study Skills Tip #1 (Appendix page 263)

Study Skills Tip #2: How to Help with Written Reports

Written reports are often difficult for students to handle in an organized manner. Study Skills Tip #2 contains three suggestions for parents that can make the job easier:

1. Use a Long-Range Planner.

2. Use a Written Report Checklist.

3. Use a Proofreading Checklist.

Each tip is accompanied by a corresponding reproducible worksheet for parents to use with their child.

Study Skills Tips #3: How to Help Your Child Study for Tests

Students can study more effectively if they learn some helpful techniques. Study Skills Tip #3 gives parents steps their children should follow when preparing for a test.

NOTE: Each study skills tip is self-contained on its own page(s) in the Appendix. Rather than send them home all at once, you may choose instead to send specific tips home in correlation with assigned work.

Keep the lines of communication open.

Throughout *Parents On Your Side*, we have emphasized the importance of consistent communication with parents. This is especially true with homework. Here are some ideas that can keep the home-school connection working effectively.

Institute a parent-teacher homework memo-line.

When you need a reply to a homework question or problem, use a parent-teacher homework memo. Write your message on the top portion of the memo; ask parents to respond on the lower part and return the memo to you. You may wish to send parents a supply of memos at the beginning of the school year, along with a letter encouraging them to write whenever they have a homework-related question that they would like to discuss with you.

Send home positive homework notes to parents.

Just as you send positive notes to parents about students' good behavior or academic success, you can also send notes home relating specifically to homework. These notes are especially effective if they relate to assignments parents have been involved with, or if they address homework problems that have been solved.

For example:

> "Just a note to let you know what a great job Austin did on his report on mammals. I know how much hard work he put in on it. Thanks so much for helping him get the library books he needed!"

> "Susan has turned in all of her math assignments during the past two weeks and she earned an A on her test today. Now she understands that doing homework makes a difference in how well she does on tests!"

As with other positive notes you send, follow these guidelines.

- Plan to send home a specific number of positive homework notes each week.

- Be specific. Tell the parent exactly what the student did to earn the note.

- Keep a record of notes sent home.

Give positive homework notes to students.
Students put lots of effort into homework. Let them know you both notice and appreciate the work they do. Pay particular attention to students who have improved their homework habits. Your praise will increase the likelihood that these new habits will continue.

> "Terrific job on your outline. I can tell that you really used your resource materials."

> "Thank you for writing so neatly. Now your stories are even more fun to read!"

Send home test update slips.
Students often forget to study for tests until the last minute. And parents sometimes hear about tests when it's too late to help their children study. Test update slips can help both student and parent

prepare for tests. Send these notices home well in advance of important tests. Have both the student and the parent sign the slips and return them to class. This form of home-school communication can be a very positive force in promoting good study habits.

Encourage the use of homework assignment books.

Assignment books ensure that students write down all homework and that parents have an opportunity to see what those assignments are. Students keep the assignment book in their notebook, take it home each day and bring it back the next day. If appropriate, you may ask parents to sign the assignment book each night, indicating that homework assignments have been completed.

Using an assignment book prevents students from saying that they don't know what their assignments are and ensures that the parents know exactly what is expected of their children each night. By involving parents with an assignment book you may solve many problems because the students know that their parents know what each night's assignments are.

For younger students, consider sending home a weekly homework calendar that lists all assignments for the week.

For example:

Room 6   Mrs. Warner
Homework for the week of March 16

	Homework	**Parent Initials**
Monday	Spelling worksheet #23	_____
Tuesday	Math worksheet	_____
Wednesday	Handwriting practice sheet	_____
Thursday	Study for spelling test on Friday	_____

Sample homework calendar

It's easy for young children to forget their homework assignments. A homework calendar gives parents a way to check what's been assigned and what their child has completed.

Ask parents to sign completed homework.
Sometimes just asking a parent to sign completed homework assignments is enough to motivate students to finish them. Use this technique whenever you want to make sure a parent is checking a student's work.

Sat Sun Assign Family Weekend Learning Activities.

Parent-child homework assignments can be worthwhile experiences for everyone. Yet few things are as frustrating to a parent as arriving home from work at night, exhausted, and finding out a child has an assignment that requires parental input . . . and is due the next day! It's not fair to the parent, and it's not fair to the student. What should be a pleasant activity instead turns into a stressful duty.

Teachers often avoid assigning homework on the weekends, but maybe it's time to reassess. After all, many parents have more time to spend on a child's work during the weekend than they do during

the week. Try this idea: Tell parents that once a month (or twice a month), students will be bringing home a weekend assignment that will involve parents in some way. Explain your reasons for these assignments:

Dear Parent(s):

Although it's important that students learn to do their homework on their own, I believe there are times when they can benefit from working with parents on a project. For this reason, I am planning to send home a variety of Family Learning Activities throughout the year. These activities are designed to involve you and your child in a creative and interesting activity. I know you are busy, so I will let you know ahead of time when each assignment is coming. I will plan these assignments for weekends when you and your child will have more time to do and enjoy them. It is my hope that these activities will be fun for everyone.

Sincerely,

Mrs. Williams

Sample letter to parents

Here are some starter ideas for Family Weekend Learning Activities:

Smart Shopper
Go to the grocery store together. Pretend you have $25.00 to spend. Your job is to plan a lunch and dinner for four people. Make sure each meal is well balanced. Write down your menu and the cost of each item you will have to buy.

Walk 'n Talk
Go on a walk in your neighborhood with your parent or another adult. Together write down ten things you see, ten things you smell, ten things you hear and ten things you touch.

Finders Keepers
Using items found around home, work with your parent to make:

• something funny to look at.

• something that can move forward.

• the tallest structure you can that still balances.

• a structure that is 4 inches high and 3 inches wide.

Speak Out!

Interview your parent to find out about _____.

For example:

• your family tree.

• his or her opinion of the United Nations.

• his or her favorite book.

• what he or she would do in case of an emergency (such as an earthquake, tornado or flood).

• his or her opinion about the best place in the world to live.

Turn It On!

Watch "Our Planet Earth" on channel 6 Saturday night.

Parent: List ten things you will do to help the environment.

Student: List ten things you will do to help the environment.

Read your lists to each other. Are any items the same? Decide on four things each of you will begin doing right away.

NOTE: In consideration of different family situations, you may wish to always offer a choice of three activities.

Help parents solve their children's homework problems.

When problems with homework persist, and you can't solve them yourself, you need more involvement on the part of parents. On Appendix pages 273-287 of *Parents On Your Side* you will find parent resource sheets you can use throughout the year to help parents deal with specific homework problems. These resource sheets offer a plan of action for parents to follow when:

• Children do not do their best work.

• Children refuse to do their homework.

• Children fail to bring assignments home

• Children take all night to finish homework.

• Children will not do homework on their own.

• Children wait until the last minute to finish assignments

• Children will not do homework if parents are not home.

Before giving parents any of the resource sheets, make sure that you read them all thoroughly. While each sheet varies slightly, they all more or less give parents the following directions for solving their child's homework problem:

The parent resource sheets explain that parents should:

1. Clearly and firmly state their homework expectations to the child.

2. Institute mandatory homework time (as explained on the resource sheets) and determine loss of privileges if the child still chooses not to do homework.

3. Give praise and positive support for work well done.

4. Provide backup incentives for continued good work.

5. Back up their words with action.

6. Contact the teacher if all else fails.

How to Use the Parent Resource Sheets

• When there is a homework-related problem you need help with, contact the parent by phone or make arrangements to get together in a face-to-face meeting.

• Together determine the specific problem the child is having with homework, for example, takes all night to get it done, forgets to bring assignments home. (Review the guidelines on pages 145-160 for conducting a problem-solving conference.)

• Select the appropriate resource sheet and together go over each of the steps to make sure the parent understands what is to be done. Then give or send the sheet home to the parents. Don't give the resource sheet to a parent if you feel he or she will be intimidated by it. Instead, make sure that the parent is given clear verbal guidelines to follow.

• Set a time (in a week or two) to follow up with the parent to determine whether the strategy has been effective or if further action is necessary.

For the parent(s) of_____

From time to time your child may forget to bring home books or homework assignments. But when he or she continually fails to bring home assigned homework, you must take action.

Here's what to do when your child fails to bring assignments home:

1 State clearly that you expect all homework assignments to be brought home.
Tell your child, "I expect you to bring home all your assigned work and all the books you need to complete your assignments. If you finish your homework during free time at school, I expect you to bring it home so that I can see it."

2 Work with the teacher(s) to make sure you know what homework has been assigned.
Students should be writing all homework assignments down on a weekly assignment sheet. Ask your child's teacher(s) to check and sign the assignment sheet at the end of class. When your child completes the assignments, you sign the sheet and have your child return it to the teacher.

3 Provide praise and support when all homework assignments are brought home.
Make sure that your child knows that you appreciate it every time he or she brings home all homework assignments. "It's great to see that you remembered to bring home all of your homework. I knew you could do it."

4 Institute Mandatory Homework Time.
If your child still fails to bring home assignments, he or she may be avoiding homework in favor of spending time with friends or watching TV. Mandatory Homework Time eliminates the advantages of forgetting homework.

Sample front page parent resource sheet

Mandatory Homework Time means that your child must spend a specific amount of time on academic activities whether homework is brought home or not. In other words, if one hour (or two) is allotted each night for homework, the entire time must be spent on academic work such as reading, or reviewing textbooks or class notes. When students learn that their irresponsible approach to homework will not be rewarded with more free time, they will quickly learn to remember to bring home their assignments.

5   Use a Homework Contract.
A Homework Contract is an effective motivator for young people of any age. A Homework Contract is an agreement between you and your child that states: "When you do your homework, you will earn a reward." For example: "Each day that you bring home your homework and complete it appropriately, you will earn one point. When you have earned five points (or ten points) you will earn a special privilege." (The younger the child, the more quickly he or she should be able to earn the reward.)

6   Work with the teacher to follow through at school for homework not completed.
If your child continues to forget homework, discuss with the teacher the possibility of imposing loss of privileges at school. Loss of lunch time, or assigning after-school detention lets your child know that you and the school are working together to ensure that he or she behaves responsibly.

Your child must learn to bring home and complete all homework assignments. Accept no excuses.

Parents and Homework Do's and Don'ts

Do

- Let parents and students know exactly how you will deal with homework. Send your homework policy home before you give the first homework assignment.

- Give parents tips for helping their children do homework

- Send home positive homework notes to parents

- Assign a homework study buddy for each student

- Let parents know about upcoming tests.

- Plan your homework when you plan your classroom lessons

- Require students to write down all homework assignments in an assignment book or on an assignment sheet.

- Make sure that all of your homework assignments are appropriate to the age and skill level of the student

- Make sure that students understand how to do each homework assignment. Explain the assignment before students go home.

- Collect and comment upon all homework. Students must know that you are paying attention to the work they do

- Whenever possible, comment in a positive way on how each student did on an assignment.

Don't

- Don't give last-minute, thrown-together homework assignments.

- Don't give homework assignments that have no objective.

- Don't give assignments that bear no connection to lessons.

- Don't expect students to know how to study unless they've been taught study skills.

- Don't overload students with homework. Be sensitive to the realities of their lives

- Don't give only drill and practice homework.

✓ Parents and Homework Checklist

Refer to this checklist as you plan your homework program.

Have you:

____Sent home a homework policy to all parents?

____Sent homework and study skills tips home to all parents?

____Planned to teach homework skills to your students?

____Set goals for yourself for sending home positive homework notes to parents?

____Set goals for yourself for sending home positive homework notes to students?

____Planned to assign Family Learning Activities throughout the year?

Chapter 8

Documenting Problems

> 66 *When it's time to present details of a problem, you need to be prepared.* 99

When it comes to their child's misbehavior, parents often resist believing what they are told. Nobody likes to hear bad news. It's especially hard for parents to hear anything negative about their child. They may feel it reflects on their parenting abilities or feel it's something they have no control over.

It will benefit both you and parents to keep accurate documentation of all academic or behavior problems as they appear. Documentation will strengthen your position as a professional, help you communicate clearly to parents and provide strong evidence to parents who may question your word.

Start right away.
Early in the school year your experience and intuition will guide you in recognizing those students who may have problems. It is vital that you begin documenting their actions immediately. Having anecdotal records will be necessary when you seek the support of administrators and parents.

Be specific.

When you write your documentation, keep away from vague opinions:

"Sean misbehaved all day long."

"Kerry didn't do anything she was supposed to today."

Base your statements on factual, observable data:

"Yesterday, Sean threw his lunch tray on the ground and shoved other children in three separate instances."

"Today during reading, Louise repeatedly jumped up and bothered her neighbor."

Consistent, specific documentation will enable you to give a non-judgemental account of a student's performance. Documentation enables you to tell parents exactly what's going on—behaviorally, academically or with homework.

Use any of the following methods for documenting student behavior.

- A small notebook with one page designated for each student. Insert a page for the student only when the first infraction occurs. Secondary teachers usually designate a documentation section for each class period.

- A 3x5 index card, alphabetically arranged in a file box, for each student.

- A loose-leaf notebook with one or more pages per student. (This is especially useful for a class with many difficult students.)

An anecdotal record should include the following information:

- Student's name and class

- Date, time and place of incident

- Description of problem

- Action taken

Johnson, Kim   Period 4

10/8 Kim cut math class. Phoned Mr. Johnson.
      Said he won't let her go out with friends if
      it happens again.

10/20 Kim cut class. Sent note to Mr. Johnson.

10/24 Kim cut class. Sent note to Mr. Johnson
      to arrange a conference. No response
      a/o 10/26.

10/30 Called Mr. Johnson. Left message to
      return call. No response.

11/20 Principal sent note to arrange conf.

Sample
3X5 index card

Lois Simon   Grade 4

Date/Time	Place	Rule Broken	Action Taken
9/15 10:45	Classroom	Refused to return to seat	Warning
9/15 1:20	Classroom	Running in class	Lose 10 minutes recess
9/15 1:40	Classroom	Called out without raising hand	Lose 20 minutes recess
9/18 2:00	Hallway	Ran out of line for drink of water	Warning
9/18 2:40	Gym	Continued playing after whistle blew	No gym next week

Sample
small
notebook

Organize and file your documentation.

Create a separate folder for each student who is having behavioral or academic problems. Include in each folder the following information:

- Student's name and class

- Home phone number

- Work phone number(s)

- Emergency phone number

What to file: Keep your anecdotal record in the file. In addition, keep copies of all correspondence you have had with parents regarding the student's problem(s). Make notes during phone calls and write down any agreements reached between you and the parent. Make copies of any letters or notes that you have sent to parents as well as copies of all notes and letters received from them. Don't leave anything to memory. Confidence comes from knowing you've done everything possible to solve a student's problem, and having the records to prove it.

Maintain your records so that you will have a complete chronological history of the student's problem(s). Later, when you need to refer to them or show them to an administrator or parent, a complete and accurate timeline of events will enable you to present the problem clearly and professionally.

Use your documentation.

Have documentation records with you when you meet with parents.

- Parents can read the specific behaviors their child engaged in.

- There will be no room to question how you handled the situation.

- There will be no chance for your word to be pitted against a student's word.

- The parents and you can address specific problems and find solutions.

In severe cases, the anecdotal record will show that the student has been given due process and will justify:

- Intervention of the principal

- Removal of the child from your class to another class

- Referral to a counselor or therapist

- Suspension

- Removal to another school

- Special education placement

REMEMBER: Having specific records of a student's problems will enable you to hold a more effective problem-solving conference. You will feel confident knowing you did everything you could to deal with the problem yourself. You will not be flustered and will not have to rely on your memory.

Tape Recording

If you are dealing with a particularly difficult situation, especially with a parent you feel may not trust you or who believes you are the cause of the problem, it may be useful to tape record your class so the parents can hear exactly how their child behaves.

There are two ways to do this:

- Do not tell the student you will be recording the class. This method allows parents to hear their child arguing, refusing to work, shouting out, etc.

- Tell the student ahead of time that you will be recording the class. Often if you tell a student that you will be tape recording the class that will be enough to improve behavior. This in itself may be a solution to the problem.

Documenting Problems Do's and Don'ts

Do

- Begin documenting problems as soon as they appear.

- Make sure your documentation relates factual, observable data.

- Use your documentation when you seek support from an administrator or parents

- Use the documentation to help you pinpoint specific problems a student is having

- Include the time, place, details of the incident and names of those involved.

- Organize your files chronologically so that you can present a clear, accurate picture of the history of the problem.

Don't

- Don't include your own opinions in your documentation.

- Don't let your documentation lapse. To be effective, you must keep consistent, up-to-date records.

☑ Documenting Problems Checklist

Refer to this checklist as you begin to document student problems.

Have you:

____Begun documenting problems as soon as they appear?

____Based your documentation on factual, observable data?

____Avoided writing down vague opinions?

____Created a documentation file for each student as the need arises?

____Included all pertinent communication and notes in the file?

____Organized your documentation chronologically?

Chapter 9

Contacting Parents at the First Sign of a Problem

❝ *Involving parents from the start will help you solve many problems before they get out of hand.* ❞

A common complaint among parents is that teachers wait too long before contacting them about a problem. It doesn't matter whether it's the first week of school, or even the first day. As soon as you become aware of an academic or behavioral problem that parents should know about, contact them. This issue is at the core of the parental involvement situation because parents can't be expected to be involved if they don't know what's going on, all of the time.

When should you contact a parent?

How do you know when you should contact a parent about a problem? Many situations are very clear: severe fighting, extreme emotional distress, a student who refuses to work or turn in homework. Don't think twice about involving parents when these situations occur. But what about the day-to-day instances that may not be so obvious? Often you simply have to use your own judgment.

If you are uncertain about contacting a parent, use the "Your Own Child" test. This test will put you in the position of the parent, and help clarify whether or not parental help is called for.

Follow these steps:

1. Assume you have a child of your own the same age as the student in question.

2. If your child was having the same problem in school as that student has, would you want to be called?

3. If the answer is yes, call the parent. If the answer is no, do not call the parent.

For example, if your own child forgot to bring his or her book to class one day, would you want to be called? Probably not. If the book was forgotten three days in a row, however, you most likely would want to know. The Your Own Child test helps you treat parents the way you would want to be treated and also serves to focus your attention on problems that need parent involvement.

The "Your Own Child" test helps you treat parents the way you would want to be treated.

You will find that by using the Your Own Child test you will increase your contacts with parents. And increasing contacts with parents means increasing the probability of parent support.

How to Contact Parents

Once you've decided that you are going to contact a parent, how are you going to get in touch? Just reach out . . .

The Telephone—Your Most Effective Communication Tool

A phone call is unquestionably the best way to contact parents when there is an issue that needs prompt attention. It's personal. It's immediate. And it gives you the opportunity to clearly explain the situation and answer any questions the parent may have.

Calling parents should not make you nervous or hesitant. You know that you are making the call in the best interests of your student, and have every right and obligation to do so. Relax. You can conduct a productive call. Planning is the key. You'll find that you can handle it if you know in advance exactly what you are going to say.

Write it down.

Remember, before you ever pick up the phone you need to outline what you are going to say to the parent. These notes will be your script for conducting the call, and the writing process will help you think through and clarify the points you want to make. Having the notes in front of you while you're speaking will keep you from getting nervous and forgetting important details.

Plan to address each of the points listed on the sample planning sheet (see next page). Fill out a sheet like this each time you prepare for a problem-solving phone call.

Parent Phone Call Worksheet

Initial Phone Call About a Problem

Teacher_____ Grade ___

Student's Name _____

Name of Parent(s) or Guardian _____

Phone number(s) _____

Date of call _____

Brief description of problem: _____

_____

Write down important points you will cover with parents.

1. Begin with a statement of concern.
2. Describe the specific behavior that necessitated your call.
3. Describe the steps you have taken to solve the problem.
4. Get parent input.
5. Present your solutions to the problem (what you will do; what you want the parent to do).
6. Express confidence in your ability to solve the problem.
7. Tell parents that there will be follow-up contact from you.

Notes: _____

_____

_____

Sample planning sheet

Parents On Your Side

By addressing these points you will find that your phone conversation will be both informative and effective. Most discipline problems can be solved through this first phone call. Let's take a closer look:

1. Begin with a statement of concern.

Your introductory statement will set the tone for the entire conversation. Remember, even though you're calling about a problem, you can still project a positive, sensitive attitude. Keep in mind that you're not calling to place blame or to complain. You're calling because you care about your student. Through your words, let the parent know that the welfare of his or her child is your utmost concern. When a parent hears this concern—and not an accusation—he or she will be much more receptive to you.

Which of these opening statements would you rather hear if you were the parent?

"Mrs. Smith (Mr. Young, etc.), I'm calling because:

- I'm not at all pleased with Ted's progress in reading."

- Linda's behavior in class is getting worse and worse."

or,

"Mrs. Smith, I'm calling because:

- I'm concerned about how little work Jess is doing."

- I'm concerned about how Brian gets along with the other students."

Notice that the statements that specifically express concern for the student and state the problem are more positive and inviting than the ones that do not.

2. Describe the specific behavior that necessitated the call.

Tell the parent in specific, observable terms what their child did or did not do. An observable behavior is one that you can watch going on, such as not following directions, talking out, not turning in assignments, or hitting a classmate. Always mention the specific behavior and the number of times the problem has occurred.

"The reason I'm concerned is:

- Seth shouted out in class seven times today."

- Lawrence refused to do any of his work in class for two days now."

- Nicole had two fights today with other students."

These specific, observable statements tell the parents exactly what happened. Avoid making vague statements that do not clearly communicate:

- "He's having problems again."

- "She's just not behaving."

- "Her attitude isn't good."

Comments such as these don't give parents any real information at all. In fact, they may miscommunicate and give the parent the impression that you do not like their child and are picking on him or her. Uninformative, negative comments will only serve to make parents defensive.

In addition, avoid making negative, judgmental comments such as:

"The reason I'm calling is:

- Your child has a bad attitude."

- Your child is mean."

- Your child is lazy."

Again, statements such as these give no valid information and will immediately alienate a parent.

3. Describe steps you have taken to solve the problem.

It's important that parents recognize that you have already taken appropriate action to deal with the situation—that you're not calling them in lieu of attempting to solve the problem yourself. Be specific. Tell them exactly what you have done.

"I discussed your child's behavior with him and reviewed the rules of our classroom discipline plan. In accordance with these rules, and the consequences for not following them, he has been last to recess twice. In addition, I have given him extra praise and positive attention when he is behaving."

"When Lynne refused to do her work in class I had her stay in my room during lunch to complete the assignment. In addition, I have spoken with her on three occasions regarding how she needs to complete her assignments. To further encourage her, I give her a point whenever she does her work. When she earns five points she can have extra free time."

"I had a conference with your son about his fighting. He was sent to the principal's office when he continued to fight, and the principal and I had a conference regarding how to help him."

4. Get parental input.

Ask the parent if there's anything he or she can add that might help solve the problem. Listen carefully to what the parent has to say. This is the time to listen for roadblocks and, if necessary, move the parent past them.

"Is there anything you can tell me that might help us solve this problem?"

5. Present your solutions to the problem.

Be prepared to tell the parent exactly what you are going to do, and what you would like the parent to do. In an initial phone call about a problem, the most important thing you can ask the parent to do is

---

let the child know that you called, and that you and the parent both are concerned about the problem.

"Here's what I will do at school: I'll continue to give Gary plenty of positive support when he does turn in homework on time. When he doesn't, he will have to complete it during detention. But most important, here's what I'd like you to do: Please tell Gary I called, and that I am concerned that he isn't turning in his homework. Tell him that you are concerned also. I want Gary to know that both of us are working together to help him do better in school.

6. Express confidence in your ability to solve the problem.
Whenever there is a problem, parents may become anxious. They need to know that they are dealing with a skilled teacher who has the confidence and the ability to work with their child to eliminate the problem. Keep the pediatrician analogy in mind. When a child is ill, a parent wants to hear the doctor say, "Don't worry. I know how to solve this problem. It will be taken care of." The last thing a parent wants to hear is, "I don't know how to handle this, but I'll do my best." Let parents know that you know what to do. Emphasize that with the parents' support you know you will get results. Your tone and attitude during this conversation should help express your confidence.

Make statements such as:

"Mr. Hill, I've worked with many children like your Tom. Don't worry. Together we will help him."

"Mrs. Jacobs, I've had a lot of experience with young people who have the same problem as Tamar. I know that by working together we will get results!"

"Mrs. Rivera, it's going to be just fine. Don't worry. I know how to handle children. I know how to motivate children like Carlos and I know that together we will get results."

7. Inform parents about follow-up contact from you.

When you tell parents that you will follow up on this conversation, you are promising that something is going to happen, that the problem is not going to be swept under the rug. Follow-up contact is vital if parents are going to believe in your commitment. It is also vital for positioning yourself to enlist their support in the future. Before ending the conversation, tell parents when they can expect to hear from you again.

"I will contact you in two days and let you know how things are going."

"I'll call you tomorrow and tell you about David's success!"

⛶ Be sensitive and alert.

Your phone call should not be a one-sided conversation. You are building a foundation for future cooperative efforts with the parent. Be sure to ask for parental input at comfortable, appropriate intervals. Don't push parents, but open the door a little for them to add any comments they may have. Then take the time to really listen to any concerns or comments they may express. Always put yourself in the parent's position and approach him or her in the manner you yourself would like to be approached. Listen for any roadblocks that might appear and help the parent move past them.

Sample Initial Phone Call About a Problem

Here's a conversation that incorporates all of the points discussed. Notice that the teacher not only gives the parent specific information but also shows plenty of professional confidence.

The teacher begins with a statement of concern and then describes the specific behavior that necessitated the call.

> ❝ Mr. Jones, this is Judy Spelling, Sandra's teacher. I'm calling because I'm concerned that Sandra has not been turning in her homework assignments. Last week she failed to turn in three math assignments and two social studies exercises. Today I did not receive another math assignment."

Now the teacher describes the steps she has already taken to solve the problem.

 I have discussed this situation with Sandra. I have reviewed the homework rules with her. She knows that her report card grade will drop if she keeps missing homework. Is there anything you would like to tell me that might help us solve this problem?"

The teacher asks for parental input. She must listen carefully to the response. If she hears a roadblock she will have to respond in a manner that moves the parent past it.

 Is there anything you can tell me that might help us solve this problem?"

The teacher now presents her solutions to the problem.

 Mrs. Jones, we need to work together to help Sandra develop better homework habits. Here's what I'd like to do. I am going to attach a slip to each assignment that goes home. Please ask to see all of her assignments each night. When she has finished the work, sign the slip. Chances are, your checking the work will be enough to motivate Sandra, but I'll also add a little extra incentive here at school. Each time I receive a completed assignment on time, Sandra will receive a point. When she earns ten points I will reward her with extra time in the library, which she does enjoy."

The teacher expresses confidence that the problem can be solved.

Mr. Jones, I'm certain that by working together we can help Sandra do a better job at school. She's a bright girl with a lot of potential. I'd like you to do one more thing. Please tell Sandra I called you and that I am concerned about this problem, and you are concerned about it, too."

Follow-up contact is arranged and the conversation concludes on an enthusiastic, upbeat note.

> I am going to call you next Monday and let you know how everything is working out. I'm sure I'll be calling with good news! In the meantime, be sure to give Sandra plenty of praise when she does her homework. Believe me, it makes a difference.
>
> I'm glad we've had this opportunity to talk. I look forward to our next conversation."

◥ Contact hard-to-reach parents.

Don't give up trying to contact a parent just because you've dialed home twice and not received an answer. You have to make every effort to reach a parent. You wouldn't accept defeat if the child were physically ill and needed his or her parents. Somehow you'd find a way to get through. Keep in mind that a problem ignored will probably only get worse, and then parents will wonder why they weren't informed earlier. Remember, it is your responsibility to take any measures needed to contact a parent.

Dear Mr. and Mrs. Johnson:

I'm writing because I'm concerned about how little work Danny has been doing at school. The last two days he has refused to do some of his assignments during class. As a result, I have had him stay in during recess to complete them. To help motivate him to do his work appropriately, I have told him he will receive a point each time he does his work in class. He knows that when he earns five points he will receive extra free time.

I would like your help in backing me up on this issue. Danny needs to know that his parents—as well as his teacher—insist that he does his work in school. Each day, I will send home a note to you, letting you know how well Danny is doing. Please sign the note and send it back with Danny the next day. I hope this will be enough to get Danny back on track. Please call me if you have any questions. Danny is an intelligent, inquisitive boy. I'm sure that by working together we can help him do a better job in school. I will contact you next Monday to talk about how he is progressing.

Sincerely,

Mr. Elwood

Here are some alternative strategies:

Contact Parents by Letter.
If you cannot reach a parent by phone, a letter home is your next option. This letter should be mailed, not sent home with the student. Be sure to include the same details you would have addressed in a phone call:

- Show your concern for the student.

- State the specific problem the student is having.

- List the steps you have taken to help the student with the problem.

- Explain what you would like the parent to do.

- Let the parent know that you are confident that, working together, the problem will be solved.

- Ask the parent to contact you by phone or note.

Contact either the father or the mother.
Teachers generally call the mother when there is a problem. Even if the father answers the phone, the teacher will often ask to speak to the mother. This reluctance to speak to the father has no place in a professional teacher's repertoire. Make as much effort to reach the father (at home or at work) as you do the mother.

When necessary, call the parent at work.
When you can't reach a parent at home by phone or through a note, your next step is to call him or her at work. Don't fall into the trap of feeling you shouldn't "bother" a parent at work. Think back to the pediatrician analogy. Would a doctor hesitate to call a parent at work about a child's medical problem? Would you hesitate to call a parent at work if the child was physically ill? Your behavioral and academic concerns about your student are every bit as important. Don't avoid action because you're afraid a parent might be angry. Make that phone call with the knowledge that it is your professional duty to do so. The assurance and competence you project when you speak with the parent will help diffuse any resentment a parent may feel.

Would you hesitate to call a parent at work if the child was physically ill?

Call the student's emergency number.
The school has on record an emergency phone number for each child. Most often it is the number of a friend or relative in the same building or down the street. Calling this number is an effective method for reaching the parent. When a neighbor rings the parent's doorbell to say the school is having a problem with his or her child, the parent will usually respond immediately.

Send a registered letter or mailgram.
A registered letter can have an enormous impact on a parent who seems to be avoiding you, or who you just can't get hold of. It emphasizes the importance of your message and also prevents a parent from saying he or she never received your communication.

◥ Follow up on initial contact.

If your child's teacher called you about a problem, wouldn't you want him or her to call again with a progress report? Wouldn't you want to know what was happening? Follow-up contact with parents is always necessary whether the problem has improved or not. Remember, you are building a relationship that you want to grow and improve throughout the year. The parent needs to know that you will not go away—that you care too much about the student to give up.

If the student's problem behavior has improved:
It is very important that you let the parent know that the student's behavior is no longer a problem and then thank him or her for the support and help given. Let the parent know that it was your teamwork that helped resolve the issue so quickly and satisfactorily. Most parents never receive positive feedback from teachers. It's a real boost when they hear that their child has improved and that they played a part in that improvement!

Follow-Up Phone Call

When making a call to parents about a student's improved behavior, be sure to include these points in your conversation:

• Point out the progress the student has made.

• Point out how the parent's cooperation helped the child.

• Tell the parent that you will continue to stay in touch.

Teacher:	Mr. Nelson, this is Ms. Jensen. I just wanted to let you know that since we last spoke, Brian has really improved his behavior. He is doing all his work. There is no arguing and no fighting. He seems much happier in class.
Parent:	That's great news. He seems happier at home, too.
Teacher:	I want to thank you for all the support you gave. By working with your son at home, and following through with disciplinary measures, you have helped him make some important changes. You should be pleased with the results.
Parent:	Thank you. I really appreciate that. It wasn't easy, but I realized from what you said that I had to do something at home in order to solve his problems at school.
Teacher:	Well, we've found out that by working together we can get results! I'll continue to stay in touch. And if you ever have any questions or concerns, please feel free to call me. Again, thanks so much for your support.

Follow-Up Letter

Although a phone call is the best way to follow up with parents, you may in some circumstances prefer to send a note home. Include the same information that you would in a call:

Dear Mr. Jackson,

Elliot has had perfect attendance all month. Thank you for cooperating with the school and for supervising him more closely. I know he will have an excellent year. Please call me if you have any concerns at all about his progress at school. I'll stay in touch with you, too.

Sincerely,

Miss Crowe

Follow-up contact if the problem has not improved.

If the problem has not improved, you must contact the parent regarding further action. The goal of this call will be to agree upon the next steps both you and the parent will take. Once again, write down what you want to say before you make the call.

Begin with a statement of concern.

Teacher: Mrs. Carroll, this is Mr. White. I'm calling because I'm worried that Terry is still continuing to fight at school.

Describe the problem behavior.

Teacher: He lost his temper again on the yard when he did not get his way in a game and he hit a child.

Describe what you have done.

Teacher: I've continued to speak with him and work with him on improving his behavior. We've also continued to bench him at recess when he does fight.

Get the parent's input.

Teacher: What did you do at home when you received notes from me about his fighting?

Parent: Well, I tried to ground him whenever I received the notes. It really doesn't work because he gets so upset. I can't even keep him in his room. He gets so worked up I can't deal with him.

Tell the parent what you will do and tell the parent what you want him or her to do.

Teacher: I feel we need to work further to help Terry. I think the best thing we can do to help him now is for you to come in and talk with me and Mr. Lowes, our principal. Mr. Lowes is very skilled at helping teachers and parents deal with children who have trouble fighting. I feel very confident that if you and I work together with him, we can all come up with a solution to help Terry stop his fighting.

Parent: Well, I hope you're right. But I don't know if anything will work. That's just the way Terry is.

Express your confidence.

Teacher: I understand how frustrated you are. That's why we have to work together to help him. As I said, Mr. Lowes and I have handled many students just like Terry, and I'm confident that we can help him have a better year. We need to use all the resources we have here at school, and Mr. Lowes is available to help us solve this problem. I'd like to meet as soon as possible. Could you come in tomorrow at 3:30?

File your notes and records.

Communication isn't complete until you've filed all notes and records pertaining to your parent contact. This includes your planning sheets, notes taken during the conversation and any follow-up data you may have. See the guidelines on page 121 for maintaining documentation records.

Ⓓ Contacting Parents at the First Sign of a Problem Do's and Don'ts

Do

- Use the "Your Own Child" test when you are unsure about contacting a parent about a problem.

- Make a phone call your first-choice means of reaching a parent.

- Make every effort to contact a parent. Don't give up after one or two tries. You can reach a parent if you really want to.

- Always write down what you want to say before you phone a parent.

- Be prepared to describe the specific behavior that is causing problems.

- Let the parent know what steps you've already taken to correct the problem.

- Be prepared to tell the parent what you are planning to do about the problem.

- Let the parent know that you're confident the problem can be solved

- Tell the parent there will be follow-up contact from you.

- Follow through with your promise!

Don't

- Don't apologize for "bothering" the parent. Remember, you are acting in their child's best interests.

- Don't hesitate to call a parent at work if you can't reach him or her at home.

- Don't try to reach the student's mother only. Contact with fathers is also important.

- Don't make vague statements about the student's behavior.

☑ Contacting Parents at the First Sign of a Problem Checklist

Refer to this checklist each time you prepare to make initial contact with a parent about a problem.

Have you:

_____Used the "Your Own Child" test to help you decide whether or not to contact a parent?

_____Written down all the points you want to cover with a parent?

_____Aggressively tried to contact hard-to-reach parents?

_____Included the student's father, as well as the mother, in problem-solving discussions?

_____Made follow-up contact whether or not the problem has improved?

_____Kept written records of all parent communication that has taken place?

_____Kept copies of all notes you sent home and received from parents?

Chapter 10

Conducting a Problem-Solving Conference

66 *Everything I do and say is geared toward the parent leaving the conference with hope and confidence.* 99

When a phone call or a note to a parent doesn't solve a problem, or if a specific problem seems to warrant it, you will need to meet in a face-to-face problem-solving conference.

What is a problem-solving conference?
A problem-solving conference is your opportunity to meet with a parent and discuss a specific problem a student is having in school. The conference gives you a chance to gather information on the problem and present it to the parent in an organized, professional manner. It also provides an opportunity for you to listen to a parent's input and use that information to help the student. The goal of the conference is for parent and teacher to agree upon a plan of action for solving the student's specific problem.

Plan the conference.

Your conference will be more successful if you take the time to plan all the issues you want to address. Here are the steps to follow:

1. Decide who will be involved in the conference.

2. Plan and write down what you will say to the parent.

3. Gather documentation.

Step 1: Decide who will be involved in the conference.

The first thing you need to consider is whether or not to include the student in a problem-solving conference. Some teachers try to include the student, others prefer not to. Use your own criteria to determine when the student's presence will be appropriate.

Here are some reasons teachers have for *not* including a student in a parent-teacher conference:

• Teachers may be concerned that the parent will not be able to openly discuss sensitive matters.
Parents are often understandably concerned about hurting the child by discussing shortcomings or problems in front of him or her.

• There may be occasions when a teacher believes that the student's presence would be highly disruptive.
This is particularly true in situations involving younger students who cannot sit still, or with older adolescents who may be hostile and verbally abusive throughout the meeting.

There are times, however, when it can be a very good idea to include a student in the conference. Here are several situations in which a student's presence may be helpful. (Keep in mind that a student's age and maturity must always be considered.)

- **Student input on the problem is needed.**

Sometimes you and the parent may need to hear the student's opinion on why he or she is having trouble in class or with homework. In addition, you may find that when teacher and parent are at a loss for solutions to a student's problem, the student himself may be able to provide an answer. The student may, for example, point out that a seating change could help, or that he or she needs to be given some specific study skills.

The student himself may be able to provide an answer.

- **Student commitment to change is needed.**

Having a student sit in on a parent-teacher conference can help make him or her aware of the seriousness of the problem. When the student sees parent and teacher taking the time to discuss the problem, he or she may be convinced that change really is needed. Many teachers find that if they are using a home-school contract (see Chapter 11), it is important to have the student be a part of the process.

Make the student aware of the seriousness of the problem.

- **You want to demonstrate that parent and teacher will work together to help the student.**

Many students, especially those involved in power struggles, try to play home and school off one another. If this is the case, it is vital that the student be present to hear both parent and teacher say that they will not tolerate the student's poor academic efforts or behavior problems. The student needs to see firsthand that the teacher and parent are a team and that there will be continued, consistent communication between home and school. The student needs to clearly understand that there will be consequences at both home and school if he or she continues to behave inappropriately.

NOTE: If you do decide that a student's presence at a conference is warranted, you may want to meet with the parent first, then at a suitable point invite the student in to continue the conference.

Team Conference

A team conference is one that involves more than one teacher. To help solve a student's problem, middle school and secondary school teachers, as well as some elementary teachers, often need to meet as a team with a parent. The goal of such a conference is not to gang up on a parent and overwhelm him or her with complaints, but to let the parent know that all of you are in this together, and that working as a team you can solve the student's problem.

Setting Up a Team Conference

In a team conference, one teacher must be designated to serve as facilitator. It will be the responsibility of this teacher to do the following:

1. Contact the parent to arrange a time for the conference.

Offer flexible time choices.

2. Conduct a pre-conference planning session.

Meeting with a group of teachers may be intimidating to a parent. It is vital that every teacher involved is in agreement ahead of time about the goals of the conference and the means of achieving these goals. The pre-conference planning session is the time to iron out these issues.

Follow these steps:

• Isolate one or two problems to be discussed.
It is not productive to overwhelm a parent with everyone's complaints about the student. You don't want to turn the meeting into a dumping session. Even if more than one problem is occurring, narrow the field down to one or two to be discussed at this particular conference.

• Coordinate documentation that will be presented.
The parent needs to see specific documentation of the student's problem behavior from each teacher involved.

• Write down all the points the team wishes to discuss.
It is important that when the team of teachers meets with a parent, you've already worked out an agenda of points to cover. Use a Problem-Solving Conference Planning Sheet (see sample on page 151) to plan what will be said. It is the responsibility of the facilitator to keep the conference focused by sticking to the points on the agenda.

Follow the guidelines given on pages 152-160 for conducting a problem-solving conference. Plan to have all members of the team contribute by addressing different points.

3. Lead the parent conference.

The facilitator must see that the conference stays on track—that the teachers stick to addressing the issues that were planned. The facilitator should also pay attention to the parent's feelings.

In a team-conference situation it is particularly important that teachers be sensitive to the parent. After all, there's only one of them and several of you. The facilitator must take special care to see that everyone listens to what the parent has to say. Above all, an atmosphere must be generated that instills confidence and optimism. Remember, your goal is to both solve the problem and take steps toward getting parent support in the future.

Take special care to see that everyone listens to what the parent has to say.

> Whatever the variation of your problem-solving conference, the final two steps remain the same.

Step 2: Plan and write down what you will say to the parent.

Before your meeting, write down the important points you want to cover with the parent. Doing so will help you develop the skill and confidence that will allow you to conduct a more productive conference. Plan to take your notes with you for referral. Doctors look at notes during a consultation. Lawyers do, too. It's perfectly acceptable, and professional, to do so. It most likely will give parents even more confidence in you. The sample Problem-Solving Conference Planning Sheet on the next page lists the points you should cover in the conference. (See pages 152-157 for a complete discussion regarding these points.) Use a planning sheet like this to prepare for each problem-solving conference you hold.

As you prepare, keep in mind how a parent is likely to be feeling at the conference. You are meeting because of a problem, so chances are the parent may be anxious, upset or worried. Be sensitive to his or her feelings. A friendly, positive atmosphere will produce more results than an intimidating setting. Once again, make a mental note to put yourself in the position of the parent. Ask yourself, "How would I feel if I were the parent in this situation?", "How would I want the teacher to treat me?" Then let that awareness guide your words and actions.

Step 3: Gather documentation.

An important part of a problem-solving conference is describing the specific problem and then presenting documentation. Parents often need to see proof that a problem does exist. Make sure you have all of your documentation with you at the conference. Have it ordered chronologically so you can present a clear picture to the parent of what has transpired.

Preparation for a problem-solving conference includes determining who will be involved, planning what to say and gathering documentation.

Problem-Solving Conference Planning Sheet

Teacher _____ Grade _____

Student's name _____

Parent(s) or Guardian _____

Date of conference _____

1. Begin with a statement of concern, updating the situation.
2. Describe the specific problem. Present documentation.
3. Describe what you have already done to solve the problem.
4. Get parental input on the problem.
5. Get parental input on how to solve the problem.
6. Tell parents what you will do to help solve the problem.
7. Explain what you need the parent to do to solve the problem.
8. Let the parent know that you're confident that the problem can be worked out.
9. Tell the parent that there will be follow-up contact from you.
10. Recap the conference.

Notes:

_____

_____

_____

Sample problem-solving conference planning sheet

Sample Problem-Solving Conference

Now let's go through a problem-solving conference, step by step.

1. Begin with a statement of concern, updating the situation.

Because a problem-solving conference can be stressful and upsetting to parents, it is important that you begin the conversation by showing your concern for the student rather than just bluntly stating the problem.

> "Mr. Smith, I'm still worried about John's misbehavior on the yard."

> "Mrs. Davis, I'm still concerned about Jenny's failure to turn in her homework assignments."

2. Describe the specific problem and present pertinent documentation.

Explain in specific, observable terms what the child did or did not do. Remember that an observable behavior is one that you can watch going on, such as not following directions, not turning in assignments or fighting on the yard. Show the parent your records that document the child's behavior.

> "This week John was involved in four fights. You can see here that he was sent to the office by yard aides twice on Tuesday and again on Wednesday and Thursday."

> "You can see from these records that Jenny did not turn in any math assignments this week."

3. Describe what you have done.

As you show your documentation, explain how you have dealt with the problem. If appropriate, refer to your classroom discipline plan and point out that you have been acting in accordance with that plan.

> "As you know, I have given John detention each time he's been involved in a fight."

"I have reminded Jenny that her final report card grade will drop if homework is not turned in. I have also sent her to detention to finish her work."

4. Get parental input on the problem.

Listen carefully to what the parent has to say. As you listen, take special care to show the parent that you respect his or her opinion. Too often, parents and teachers don't show respect to one another. As a professional, it's up to you to take the lead by showing parents you value what they say. (Use the effective listening techniques outlined on pages 158-160.)

Here are some questions you may want to ask:

"Has your child had similar problems in the past?" (It may be useful to examine school records to determine if the child did have problems previously and if the parent was aware of them.)

"Does your child have similar problems at home?"

"Why do you feel your child is having such problems?"

"Is there something going on at home that could be affecting your child's behavior (divorce, separation, siblings, a move)?"

5. Get parental input on how to solve the problem.

Most parents know their child better than anyone. They just may have a good idea about how to solve a specific problem. Chances are, you'll hear something like, "Well, I guess I'll have to do something to make sure he behaves in school." That's your opportunity to move in and enlist their help. Seize the moment!

Ask the parent:

"How do you feel we can work together to help your child solve this problem?"

6. Tell the parent what you will do to help solve the problem.

You've already explained what you have previously done, and what effect it has had. Now explain your new plan of action to resolve this issue. Let the parent know exactly what you are going to do. Then check for understanding to make sure everything is clearly understood.

> "Mr. Smith, since this problem has continued, I am going to change the disciplinary consequences for John. From now on, each time he fights on the yard he will be sent immediately to the principal and you will be called. He won't receive any warnings first, and he won't be sent to detention."

> "Mrs. Davis, since the problem wasn't solved, I am going to develop a behavior contract for Jenny. Every time she doesn't turn in homework she will go to detention. Every time she does turn in her homework she will receive a point. Ten points and she's earned a bonus grade."

Note: If there is to be Home-School Contract, introduce it now. (See Chapter 11 for complete guidelines.)

7. Explain what you need the parent to do to solve the problem.

Now you must explain, just as carefully, what you would like the parent to do to help solve the problem. As you speak and listen, pay close attention to any roadblocks that might appear (does the parent sound overwhelmed? negative? confused?). Use your communication skills to move the parent past the roadblock. Make sure the parent understands exactly what you are asking.

> "Mr. Smith, we need to work together to help John improve his behavior. His fights on the yard are completely unacceptable. Any time you are called about a fight, I'd like you to follow through at home with your own disciplinary measures. Taking away privileges often works to convince kids that you mean business. Whatever you choose to do, remember that you must do it consistently and not back down."

"Mrs. Davis, it is extremely important that we work together to help Jenny get into the habit of turning in all her homework assignments. To do this, I would like you to check each night to see that all assignments are completed. Your signature on her homework will show me that you've looked it over. Please understand, I don't expect you to correct the work, just make sure it's complete."

8. Let the parent know you're confident that the problems can be worked out.

Well-chosen words will punctuate your message with assurance:

- Use the word "confident" when you speak to the parent.

- Use both the parent's name and the student's name.

- Reassure the parent that you are experienced in dealing with this type of problem.

"Mr. Smith, I am confident that together we can make this a better year for John. I've dealt with many children who have had this problem, and I can assure you that we will be able to turn things around if we are united in our efforts."

"Mrs. Davis, I feel confident that with both of our efforts we can help Jenny develop more responsible homework habits."

9. Tell the parent that there will be follow-up contact from you.

A parent needs to know that you are going to stay involved. Provide this reassurance by giving a specific date for a follow-up call or note.

"Mr. Smith, I am going to call you next Monday evening to let you know how things are working out for John."

"Mrs. Davis, I'll give you a call Friday night to let you know how the week went."

10. Recap the conference.

Write down all agreed-upon actions. Whenever communication takes place, there is always the question of whether each party understands what the other is saying. To avoid confusion and assure that the message was clear, you may need to clarify all agreements. You can do this by restating and writing down what you are going to do and what the parent is going to do. Keep this information in your files. If you feel it will be helpful to the parent, tell him or her that you will mail a copy of this agreement home in a day or two.

Teacher: We've agreed to a number of things today. Just to make sure we're both clear about what we're going to do, I'm going to write the important points down. Here's what I've agreed to do: I am going to change the disciplinary consequences for John. From now on, each time he fights on the yard he will be sent immediately to the principal and you will be called. No more warnings. No more detention.

The teacher writes while speaking.

Now, what are the steps you're going to take?

Parent: Any time that I'm called about John fighting, I'll take privileges away from him at home. And I'll do it every time, not just once in awhile.

The teacher continues writing.

Teacher: OK, I've got it all written down. Mr. Smith, I'd like to thank you for helping me put this plan of action together. Now John will know that we're working together to solve this problem.

Another example:

Teacher: OK, Mrs. Davis. We've agreed to a plan of action here today that will help Jenny do a better job on homework. Here's what I will be doing: I'm going to develop a behavior contract for Jenny. Every time she doesn't turn in homework she will have detention. Every time she does turn in her homework she will receive a point. Ten points and she will earn a bonus grade.

To be certain that we both understand what will be happening, I'm going to write down what both of us have agreed to do.

The teacher begins writing.

Now, what will you be doing each night to help Jenny handle homework better?

Parent: Every night, I'm going to check all of Jenny's completed homework. And I'll sign each paper to show you that I've seen it.

The teacher continues writing.

Teacher: That's going to be really helpful. When you check her homework each night, Jenny will better understand that both of us are committed to her success in school. I'm sure we'll soon see a difference in her homework habits.

Closing the Conference

Thank the parent for coming in to meet with you. Let him or her know that taking the time to improve the child's educational experience is time well spent.

Conference Communication Tips

Here are some useful communication techniques you can implement in any parent conference.

Use Effective Listening Skills

A successful face-to-face conference depends on more than what you are prepared to say. It also depends upon how you listen and react to what a parent says. You can't anticipate a parent's words, but the following techniques will help you show parents that you respect and accept their feelings.

Non-Verbal Techniques

- Lean forward toward the parent when he or she is speaking. This shows you are interested in what is being said.

- Maintain eye contact. You can't really listen to someone if you aren't looking at him or her.

- Maintain open body posture. Do not cross your arms. Instead, show openness and a willingness to listen.

- Make sure there are no physical barriers between you and the parent. It's best to sit next to each other at a table. Don't sit at your desk with the parent on the other side.

- You must be willing to sit quietly and listen to what the parent has to say. Don't take over the conversation. Feel free to add some verbal assurances ("I understand," etc.) to show you are listening, but avoid interrupting.

Reflective Listening

It is important, especially if a parent is upset, that you show you empathize with what he or she is saying. A technique called reflective listening is very effective for doing this. When you use this technique, you simply reflect back in words the fact that you heard what the parent said and understand how he or she feels. You are not making a judgement about what is being said. You are not agreeing or disagreeing. You are simply letting the parent know that you hear and you understand. This is a powerful technique that will demonstrate to a parent that you respect the feelings he or she is expressing.

For example:

Parent: I don't know what to do with that boy. He just won't listen to me.

(reflective response)
Teacher: I hear how upset you are about your son.

Preface your reflective response with comments such as "I under-stand," or "I hear."

"I hear how upset you are."
"I understand how upset you are about all of this."

Here are some sample comments from parents, with the teacher's reflective response:

Parent: I honestly believe his problems are caused by other children.

(reflective response)
Teacher: I hear how upset you are.

Parent: You need to understand that I'm a single mom. I work. I don't have any time to deal with this.

(reflective response)
Teacher: I understand how overwhelmed you feel.

Parent: I fight every night with him to try to get him to do his homework.

(reflective response)
Teacher: I hear how frustrated you are.

Parent: I really don't know if she should be held back.

(reflective response)
Teacher: I hear how confused you are.

Reflective listening is a valuable skill. Combined with effective nonverbal techniques it can greatly increase your ability to communicate with parents.

When you are using a translator. . .

You may need to use the services of a translator during a conference. Here are a few important guidelines to keep in mind:

- Sit facing the parent, with the translator seated next to you.

- As you speak, always look directly at the parent, never at the translator. When the translator speaks, continue to look at the parent.

- Keep your eyes on the parent when he or she speaks, not on the translator. Continue to do so when the translator speaks.

In other words, make sure that the conference is between you and the parent, not you, the parent and the translator. Pay attention to your body language. Lean forward as you speak. Maintain eye contact and through your gestures and attitude exude a warmth and caring that will transcend spoken words.

Conducting a Problem-Solving Conference Do's and Don'ts

Do

- When appropriate, offer the parent assistance in disciplining his or her child. See Chapter 12 for more specific guidelines.

- Use effective listening techniques throughout the conference

- Bring documentation with you to the conference

- Be sensitive to a parent's feelings throughout the conference. Listen carefully and make comments to demonstrate that sensitivity

- Consider whether or not you want the student to be present at the conference.

- Explain problems to parents in observable terms. Be specific.

- Give parents the materials they need to support your plan of action: stickers, checklists, award certificates

- Leave parents with hope and confidence!

Don't

- Don't arrive at the conference unprepared. Make sure you have written down all the points you want to cover.

- Don't have a parent sit on a student-sized chair while you sit in the teacher's chair.

- Don't dredge up incidents from the past.

- Don't overwhelm parents by presenting too many problems. Two or three examples are enough.

- Don't make idle disciplinary threats.

- Don't talk about other students if the parent tries to divert the conversation by placing blame on others.

✔ Conducting a Problem-Solving Conference Checklist

Refer to this checklist each time you prepare for a problem-solving conference.

Have you:

____Written down what you will say to the parent at the conference?

____Decided what you will do to help solve the problem?

____Decided what you want the parent to do?

____Reminded yourself to listen to what the parent says-to treat him or her with respect?

____Organized the documentation you need to bring to the conference?

____Reviewed effective listening skills?

____Decided whether or not to include the student in the conference?

If the conference involves more than one teacher, **have you:**

____Designated one teacher to be the facilitator?

____Arranged to hold a pre-conference planning meeting with all teachers involved?

____Gathered documentation from all teachers involved?

____Decided, with the other teachers, on one or two problems to focus on?

____Written down what will be said to the parent at the conference?

Using a Home-School **11**
Contract

66 *Parents are full of good intentions during a conference. But once they're back home it may be a different story.* 99

It's one thing for a parent to agree at a conference to work with you to solve a student's specific problem. It's sometimes quite another to actually succeed at making this partnership work. After the conference is over, after the parent goes home, how do you ensure success? How do you make certain that you meet the goals you and the parent set during the conference? How can you make certain you get the support you need?

The best way to successfully structure a parent's efforts with you is by using a home-school contract.

What is a home-school contract?

A home-school contract is a written agreement between teacher, student and parent. The contract states that the student agrees to a specific behavior. If the student complies with the terms of the contract, he or she will earn praise and rewards from both the teacher and parent.

The success of a home-school contract demands that both parent and teacher consistently enforce it.

Be sure that the student understands that both parent and teacher are working together in a team effort to solve a problem. The student knows that if he or she chooses not to comply with the contract, he or she can expect predetermined negative consequences from both school and home. The success of a home-school contract demands that both parent and teacher consistently enforce it. A home-school contract is an effective technique to use with both elementary and secondary school students.

Home-School Contract

Jeffrey Smith promises to stay out of fights on the schoolyard. Each day the student does as agreed, he/she can expect the following actions to take place.

From the teacher:
1. Praise.
2. One point for each day of appropriate behavior. When ten points are earned, Jeffrey may spend an extra hour on the computer.
3. A note home to parents telling them of Jeffrey's successful day.

From the parent:
1. Praise.
2. One point for each day of appropriate behavior. When ten points are earned Jeffrey may invite a friend to dinner and a movie.

Each day the student does not do as agreed, he or she can expect the following actions to take place.

From the teacher:
1. Fifteen minutes detention after school.
2. A note home to parents telling them about Jeffrey's behavior that day.

From the parent:
1. Loss of TV and phone privileges that night.

Contract will be in effect from October 6 to October 17.

_____

Parent signature   Teacher signature   Student signature

Sample home-school contract

When should you use a home-school contract?

Use this technique to correct behavioral, academic or homework problems for any age level. A contract is warranted when you can answer yes to any of these questions:

- Could the student benefit from a structured system of positive and negative consequences?

- Does the parent need daily feedback regarding the student's behavior at school?

- Have you tried to solve the problem through other means, without success?

- Do you suspect that the student receives little positive reinforcement at home?

- Has a student's parent asked for help from you in solving a student's problem?

Why is a home-school contract effective?

A home-school contract helps the teacher, parent and student focus on a specific problem that needs to be solved. Vague comments like "He's always getting into trouble" or "Her behavior is just impossible" don't help a problem get solved. You need to pinpoint exactly what behavior you want from a student. The home-school contract will help you and the parent do just that.

A home-school contract requires parent and teacher to decide upon steps they will both take to solve the problem. A home-school contract is really a plan of action for helping a student improve his or her behavior. It helps structure disciplinary responses for parents who don't know what to do to help their child.

A home-school contract encourages the parent to positively reinforce his or her children for appropriate behavior. Many students, particularly those with behavior or academic problems, just don't hear enough good things about themselves from parents. When a teacher meets with a parent and writes a contract that stipulates parental positive reinforcement, he or she is really teaching the parent about the value and benefits of positive reinforcement.

A home-school contract requires the parent to state, in writing, that he or she agrees to fulfill the obligations of the contract. Teachers' attempts to solve a student's problem often fail because parents don't carry through at home with both positive support and negative consequences. The home-school contract gives parents a framework to follow and gives teachers a means of keeping track of what's going on at home. Once the parent signs the agreement, the teacher is within his or her rights to inquire if the parent is following through as planned.

Keep in mind that the effectiveness of the contract depends greatly on how well it is written and explained to the parent. A home-school contract is not a prefabricated document to be taken out and used in any situation with any student. It is a very personal agreement, custom-tailored to meet the needs of a particular student and parent. For the contract to be effective, the positive reinforcement and negative consequences must be geared to the specific student and the realities of his or her parent(s).

How to Write and Present a Home-School Contract

A home-school contract is a collaborative effort between teacher and parent, and should be dealt with as part of a problem-solving conference. Here are the steps to explaining and writing a home-school contract:

Step 1: Introduce the concept of a home-school contract to the parent.

A careful explanation of the contract is vital. Chances are the parent has never even seen one before. Explain right away that the contract is an agreement between you, the parent and the student, and that the purpose of the contract is to help the student succeed in school. Be sensitive. Once again, put yourself in the parent's position and realize that this procedure at first might seem a bit intimidating. Let the parent know that you have successfully used home-school contracts before.

I feel that the best way to help *(student's name)* is for us to put together a home-school contract for him (her). A home-school contract is a written agreement between me, you and your child. The contract will state that *(student's name)* agrees to a specific behavior. If he complies with the terms of the contract, he will earn praise and rewards from both you and me. If he chooses not to comply with the contract, he will receive predetermined negative consequences from both school and home.

"The reason a home-school contract can be so successful is that your child will know that we're working together to help him solve his problem. Whenever he misbehaves during the day, I'll let you'll know about it so you can deal with it at home that night. Likewise, when he behaves appropriately, you'll know about that, too, and give him plenty of praise.

"I've used home-school contracts many times in the past and have found them to be successful.

"This is the contract form. *(Show it to the parent and let him or her look it over.)* We're going to fill this form out together now."

Step 2: Determine how you want the student to behave.

Work with the parent to focus on one or two specific areas of concern. (These should be the same problems that you presented to the parent at the beginning of the problem-solving conference.) For example: "I'm concerned about Jeffrey's fighting on the yard"; I'm very concerned that Serena is still not completing her homework assignments."

Let's begin the contract by focusing on exactly what we need your child to do at school. We've been talking about his problems with (state problem). That's the behavior we want to change. That's what this contract is all about. We will write down on the contract that (student's name) will promise to (state desired behavior). Do you have any questions about this?"

Step 3: Explain the negative consequences you will provide if the student does not comply.

You must decide on negative consequence(s) the student will receive at school if he or she chooses not to do what is expected. You should determine these consequences before the parent arrives for the conference. Explain to the parent that you will give these consequences each time the student does not comply with the contract.

 I want your child to clearly understand that we cannot allow him to continue a behavior that's not in his best interests. Therefore, I want to spell out exactly what I will do if he chooses not to follow the promise made in the contract. Here's what will happen at school:

"Each time he does not comply with the contract he will stay after school for detention. In addition, of course, a note will go home letting you know what happened.

"Now I'm going to write these consequences in the contract."

Step 4: Help the parent choose the negative consequences he or she will provide if the student does not comply with the contract.

The success of the home-school contract depends upon the parent's willingness to follow through at home. This means a parent must be willing to give negative consequences if the student does not follow the terms of the contract. Be aware that this is often difficult for parents to do effectively. At most, their disciplinary measures are probably extremely inconsistent. (Refer to Chapter 12 for suggestions on how to help parents deal more effectively with their children.)

Parents must let their child know that they will not tolerate misbehavior at school. This part of the contract is vital. You must impress upon parents the importance of consistent follow-through.

> The next thing we need to include in the contract is very important. We need to spell out exactly what you will do at home if (student's name) misbehavior continues. I can give your son detention from now until the end of the school year and it might not make a bit of difference to him. You, however, are in a position to take steps that will matter. You need to choose a negative consequence that he will receive each time he misbehaves. Choose something that you know he won't like. Parents often choose consequences such as loss of TV or phone privileges, grounding, or restricted use of a bicycle or other sports equipment. Think for a minute about what you might choose.

(Discuss options if the parent is unsure.)

> "Now let's write down on the contract the negative consequences you will use."

Step 5: Explain the positive consequences *you* will give to the student for appropriate behavior.

Motivating students to change their behavior requires positive reinforcement. A home-school contract must specify the positives that you the teacher will provide at school when the student behaves appropriately.

The best form of positive support, particularly for younger students, is verbal praise. You must include in the contract that you will consistently give the student that reinforcement when he or she complies with the terms of the contract. In addition to praise, you should consider providing the child with additional reinforcement. Think about what the student would like to earn. What would motivate him or her to give that extra bit of effort? Decide on the positive reinforcement you intend to use before meeting with the parent. (You may even want to ask the student what he or she would like to earn. The more involved the student is in this process, the more success you will have.)

Here are some positive reinforcement ideas:

Positive Reinforcement for Elementary Students:

- Healthy snacks (raisins, peanuts)

- Class monitor

- First in line

- Lunch with teacher

- Free reading time

- Extra computer time

- Choose PE activity

- Award certificate

- Stickers

Positive Reinforcement for Middle and Secondary Students:

- Extra computer time
- Gift certificate from a fast-food restaurant

- Free admission to a school function

- Right to be first to leave class

- Gift certificate from school store

I feel very strongly that your child knows that I will reinforce him when he behaves appropriately. Here's what I plan to do. Whenever he does what we have asked him to do, I will praise him and let him know that I recognize and appreciate what he has done. I want him to feel proud of his achievement and to understand that appropriate behavior will earn attention. In addition, I will give him an extra incentive. I know that your son would like to earn extra time on the computer. Each day he complies with the contract, I will give him a point. When he gets five points he will earn fifteen minutes of computer time. I think he will want to work toward this reward. Do you agree?

"Now let's fill in these provisions on the contract."

Step 6: Help the parent choose the positive reinforcement he or she will provide when the child complies with the contract.

Parents need to understand that their words of praise and support are very important to their child. Emphasize clearly that the parent really is the most important person in a child's life and that his or her praise means a lot.

66 I've told you about the positive reinforcement I will give *(student's name)* each day that his behavior improves at school. It's just as important that you give positive reinforcement at home, too. Remember, you are the most important person in his life. He really does care about what you think of him. Your words of praise can do so much in encouraging him to continue his efforts. Don't ever underestimate it! I would like to write down on the contract that each day your son behaves, you promise to give him lots of well-deserved praise.

"In addition, you may find that it would help to give an extra special reward for good behavior. Choose something that you know your child would like, and that you are comfortable giving. You may want to do the same thing I'm doing at school. Each day he behaves appropriately he will earn a point from you. When he earns five points he receives the reward. Keep in mind that the gift of your own time might be the most valuable reward you can give. Lots of students really enjoy earning special time alone with Mom or Dad.

"Here are some ideas that kids often appreciate: *(Give parent some age-appropriate suggestions. Be sensitive to his or her financial circumstances.)*

- Go out for lunch with Mom or Dad.
- Have a friend over for dinner.
- Stay up late one night.
- Go out to dinner.
- Buy a new book.
- Spend an hour of uninterrupted time with Mom or Dad."

Step 7: Decide on the duration of the contract.

You need to decide how long a contract will be in effect: one week, two weeks or three weeks. Consider the age of your student and the behavior you are dealing with. Fill this information in on the contract.

Step 8: Sign and present the contract.

The home-school contract must be signed by all involved parties: student, teacher and parent. At this point, the student may be included in the conference. Carefully explain the terms of the contract to him or her. Make sure that you and the parent present the contract together, clarifying the fact that you're working as a team.

Show a warm, positive attitude here. Let the student know that you regard the contract as an opportunity to change things for the better, not as a punishment.

As you know, your mother (father) and I are very concerned about (*state the problem*). You have received detention many times, but the problem hasn't been solved.

"We have put together a contract that will help you behave appropriately at school. This contract is an agreement between you, your mother and me about what will happen when you do and do not behave.

"Let's read it together.

(Read the terms of the contract, making sure the student understands every point.)

> As you can see, when you sign this contract you agree to *(state desired behavior)*. Each day that you behave according to the contract, you will receive *(state your positive reinforcement)* from me at school and *(state parent's positive reinforcement)* from your mother at home. On the other hand, on days that you do not comply with the contract you can expect to receive *(state your negative consequences)* from me at school and *(state parent's negative consequences)* from your mother at home. Your mother has agreed to follow through with these consequences because she cares about you and wants you to succeed at school.
>
> "This is how the contract will work: Each day, I will be sending home a note to your mother telling her how the day went. If everything went well, that is, if you behaved according to the contract, I will tell her so. If the day did not go well, I'll tell her that, too. Do you have any questions you'd like to ask me or your mother?"

Before closing the conference, make sure once again that everyone clearly understands the terms of the contract. Reassure the parent that the next day he or she will receive a note from you updating the student's progress. End the meeting on a positive, enthusiastic note. Everyone should know that you expect success!

Home-School Contract Daily Contact Sheet

Student's name _____

Date _____

Dear _____

____Today your child behaved according to the terms of the contract. I have given the positive reinforcement that we agreed upon. Please follow through at home with your positive reinforcement, also.

____Today your child did not behave according to the terms of the contract. I have given the negative consequences that we agreed upon. Please follow through at home with your negative consequences also.

Please get in touch with me if you have any questions or would like to talk about the contract.

Sincerely,

Additional comments: _____

_____

_____

Sample home-school contract daily contact sheet

◻ Daily communication is a must.

Once you've filled out and signed the contract, you need to decide how you will communicate with parents. In order to enforce the terms of the contract you will need to be in daily contact with parents. The best method of daily communication is a home-school note. Each day the contract is in effect send home a note letting the parent know how the student behaved in school that day. Include in your note:

• Date

• How the student behaved that day

• Actions you took (positive reinforcement or negative consequences)

• What the parent needs to do at home (positive reinforcement or negative consequences)

Ⓓ Using a Home-School Contract Do's and Don'ts

Do

- Use a home-school contract when you want to ensure a parent's continuing involvement in solving a student's problem.

- Write the contract with the parent.

- Decide ahead of time which positives and negative consequences you will use.

- Prepare to give the parent guidelines and suggestions for choosing the positive and negative consequences he or she will use.

- Think carefully about how you will present the concept of a contract to a parent. Make notes on what you will say.

- Be sure to emphasize to the parent how important his or her praise and support is to the child. Consistent follow-through is the key to making the contract work.

- Send home a note each day telling the parent how the student behaved.

- Always follow through on your positives and negatives. When the student behaves appropriately, he or she deserves lots of praise.

Don't

- Don't feel that using a home-school contract is asking too much of a parent. This kind of structured involvement is exactly what many parents need to help them discipline their child at home for misbehavior at school.

- Don't hesitate to call a parent any time you have a question regarding follow-through at home. If you have a feeling that the parent isn't living up to the terms of the contract, give him or her a call. Remember, the parent's signature constitutes a promise of action. Likewise, don't hesitate to call with good news, either. A parent will be most happy to hear from you when things are improving!

☑ Using a Home-School Contract Checklist

Refer to this checklist when you prepare to use a home-school contract.

Have you:

____ Decided on the specific behavior you want from the student?

____ Decided before the conference on the positive consequences you will include on the contract?

____ Decided before the conference on the negative consequence you will include on the contract?

____ Reviewed the guidelines for writing a home-school contract?

____ Made some notes about what you will say to the parent(s)?

Chapter 12

Helping Parents Support Your Disciplinary Efforts

66 *If misbehavior at school also meant loss of privileges at home, we'd see fewer behavior problems in the classroom.* 99

No matter what efforts you make at school, without parent support it will be very difficult for you to get some of your students to behave appropriately. Unfortunately, the parents of many of these students are unable to discipline their own children. To increase their ability to support you at school, you may need to give them some simple techniques to use at home.

179

As a teacher, you have been trained to use behavior management techniques in the classroom. Parents can use these same common-sense techniques to motivate their own children to behave in school. In this chapter you are given five techniques that parents can use at home. The techniques are simple and straightforward. Used correctly, they give parents the tools they need to encourage appropriate behavior from their children.

Please note the following qualifications:

• Parents must want your help. Do not give parents advice on behavior management unless they have indicated to you that they want to hear your suggestions.

• Do not work with parents on your own if you suspect the child or parent has emotional problems. Keep in mind that you are not a therapist or counselor and that it is not appropriate for you to intervene on your own in circumstances that require professional help. If you suspect that a student, or a parent, needs counseling, involve the school psychologist, counselor and/or principal.

The techniques we will be examining here are simple and effective. You can present them in only a few minutes in person or over the phone. The five techniques are:

1. Clearly tell your child exactly how you expect him or her to behave at school.

2. Avoid arguments. Use the Broken-Record technique.

3. Back up your words with disciplinary actions.

4. Know what to do when your child begins testing you.

5. Catch your child being good.

Before we demonstrate how to present these techniques to parents, let's take a closer look at each one:

1. Clearly tell your child exactly how you expect him or her to behave at school.

The first skill parents must learn is to clearly communicate how they expect their child to behave at school. Most parents who have trouble disciplining their children do not speak assertively. Instead, these parents beg, plead, threaten or become hostile.

A parent must recognize the difference between assertive responses to a child and non-assertive or hostile responses.

These responses do not get results; they do not help teach a child to behave appropriately. A parent must learn to recognize the difference between assertive responses to a child and non-assertive or hostile responses.

2. Avoid arguments. Use the Broken-Record technique.

Parents often fall into the trap of arguing with their child whenever they ask them to do anything. A technique called the Broken Record (demonstrated in the sample conversation on page 184) can help these parents avoid fruitless arguments.

With this technique the parent keeps repeating what he or she wants until the child stops arguing. The Broken Record can help a parent avoid being dragged into a pointless debate and helps focus the child on the desired behavior.

Avoid being dragged into a pointless debate.

3. Back up words with disciplinary action.

Parents need to understand that simply demanding their child to behave at school (even when it's done assertively) may not be enough to ensure that it happens. Parents must learn to back up their words with actions to let the child know they mean business—that they are serious about the child changing his or her behavior. This means that a parent must be willing to impose negative consequences when the child chooses to misbehave. If the parent doesn't follow through, the child may not either.

---

4. Know what to do when your child begins testing you.
When parents begin setting limits, and backing up their words with actions, the child will often try to manipulate the parent into backing down by crying, getting angry, or becoming defiant. It's a good idea to prepare parents for this possibility, and tell them how to handle it.

5. Catch your child being good.
As a teacher, you know that negative consequences can stop an unwanted behavior, but that positive reinforcement is the key to changing behavior. Parents need to understand that it's just as important for them to give positive reinforcement at home as it is for you to give it at school. Unfortunately, many parents who are frustrated with their children's behavior are also very negative in how they relate to their children. It is vital that parents understand that they must balance their disciplinary consequences

Parents must understand that they must balance their disciplinary consequences with positive reinforcement.

with positive reinforcement if they are ever going to teach their child how to behave in a more positive manner in school. This is a very critical point that must be explained carefully.

Introduce support techniques to parents.

Begin by showing the parent that you are sensitive to his or her situation. Let the parent know that he or she isn't alone in needing help and that you are confident that, working together, the disciplinary problems at school will be worked out. Keep in mind that many parents who have trouble with discipline are single parents facing enormous pressure in their lives. Be sensitive to this. Address the realities of their lives. The manner in which you approach this discussion will greatly affect its outcome.

"Your situation is not uncommon. Many parents today have trouble motivating their children to behave at school. And it's especially difficult when they are doing it on their own, as you are. I want to assure you that I have worked with many parents who are dealing with the same problems that you are. I'm going to give you some ideas that are easy to use and really work. I know they'll help you. They've helped a lot of other parents."

Start by explaining the need to tell the child exactly how he or she is expected to behave.

"Many parents just aren't firm when it comes to talking to their own child. This means that they aren't clear and direct about what they want their child to do. Instead, they beg or plead with them. Or else they threaten to punish them, but don't follow through. Let me show you what I mean. Here are some examples of how not to get the behavior you need:

"Please stop what you're doing. I just can't take it any more."

"How many times do I have to talk to you about your behavior?"

"Why won't you do what you're told?"

"If you do that again, you'll stay in your room all weekend."

"In each of these examples, the parent is sending a vague, emotional message, not a clear, specific one. Because of this, the child is left without direction. In addition, frustrated parents often lose their temper and end up screaming and yelling at their children. That won't get you what you need, either.

"Here's how to get what you need: You must sit down with your child and in a no-nonsense, serious manner let her (or him) know that you are the parent. And that means you set the rules. You must look your child in the eye and say: 'There is no way I am going to tolerate your misbehavior at school. I know that you can behave. And I care about you and love you too much to allow you to continue acting this way at school.'

"It is very important that you remain calm when speaking to your child. Don't yell or scream your demands. Speak in a firm, calm tone of voice. By staying calm you will let your child know that you are in control."

Now explain to the parent what to do when the child argues back.

When you tell your child to do something, chances are you'll get an argument back. Arguing is not useful. Nobody wins. You must stick to your point and let your child know you mean business. I'm going to give you a technique that parents and teachers have found to be very effective. It's called the Broken Record because when you use it you sound like a broken record that keeps repeating the same thing over and over. When you learn to use this technique you will be able to clearly tell your child what you want and not get trapped into arguments that go nowhere.

"Here's how to use the Broken-Record technique. First, tell your child exactly what you want her to do. For example, 'I expect you to do your assignments during class.'

"If your child argues, just keep repeating what you want. Do not respond to anything your child says. Just say, 'I understand, but I want you to complete your assignments during class.'

"Use the Broken Record a maximum of three times. If it does not work, stop the conversation and do not engage the child in further discussion. If the problem persists, you will have to take stronger actions, which we'll discuss next."

Explain the importance of backing up words with actions.

> If your child chooses to continue to misbehave, you must be ready to back up your words with actions. This means that you must have disciplinary consequences chosen that you will use if your child still does not behave.

"Here are some ideas to help you make sure that the disciplinary consequences you choose and use will be ones that are meaningful to your child:

"The consequence must be something that your child does not like, but it must never be physically or psychologically harmful. Taking away privileges, such as watching TV, using the computer, talking on the phone, or using the car is often effective. So is grounding. With younger children grounding can mean being restricted to their room without TV for a specific amount of time. For older children grounding can mean having to stay at home for a certain number of days.

"Here are some guidelines to follow when you give disciplinary consequences:

"Always present the consequence as a choice. Your child must understand that she has a choice. She can behave as you ask, or misbehave and choose to accept the consequence. Tell your child, 'If you misbehave at school, you will choose to (for example) lose the privilege of watching TV during the week.' You can see that in this way you are making your child responsible for her own choices.

"Give the consequence each time the child chooses to misbehave. Consistency is the key to backing up your words with action. Your child must know that you mean business. Each time your child chooses to misbehave, she must be given the consequence. No exceptions. No excuses. As soon as you back down you've lost your credibility.

"Stay calm when you give the consequence. Stay in control. Remember, your child chose this to happen. You are simply following through with what you promised.

"Forgive and forget. Once your child has received the consequence, the issue is over and should be forgotten. It's time to move on. Don't stay angry or resentful. Instead, let your child know that you still have confidence in her ability to behave appropriately."

Now explain how to handle a child who begins testing the parent.

 Children often test their parents to see if they really mean business. Don't be surprised if this happens to you. When given a consequence, your child may cry, scream or yell at you, or beg you for just one more chance. You must stand your ground. No matter what your child pulls out of his or her bag of tricks, you must follow through with the consequence. Don't give in, no matter how upset your child gets. Let your child know that you are prepared to follow through. Tell your child, for example, 'You have chosen to be restricted to your room. You will go to your room and stay there no matter how loud you yell or how long you cry.'"

Finally, and, most important, emphasize the importance of positive reinforcement.

We've been talking about giving your child disciplinary consequences whenever she chooses to misbehave. That's the tough part. The next thing you must make sure you do is a lot more fun for you and your child. And it's really the most important part of getting your child to behave. You have to give your child praise and positive support when she behaves at school. Remember, you really are the most important person in your child's life. You might be surprised at how much your praise means to her. Here's how to do it:

First, give your child plenty of praise when she begins to show improvement. You need to clearly let her know that you recognize the good effort she is making. Don't ever let a day of good behavior go unrecognized.

Tell your child:

"I like how well you did at school today. I'm so proud of you for trying so hard."

"Next, keep in mind that praise alone isn't always enough to motivate a child to improve his or her behavior. Sometimes it's helpful to combine your praise with special privileges or rewards, like staying up late one night, using the car, going out to lunch—whatever your child might appreciate (and you are comfortable giving). Ask yourself, "What would my child like to earn? What special treat might make her put in a bit more effort?

Whatever privilege or reward you pick, you must give it to your child consistently. Your child must know that, just as she can expect a disciplinary consequence for inappropriate behavior, she can also expect lots of praise and reinforcement for good behavior."

Give parents tip sheets.

On Appendix pages 289-292 you will find tip sheets containing guidelines for using the techniques discussed in this chapter. Give these sheets to parents after you have discussed their use in a conference or phone call. Do not give or send these tip sheets to parents who have not expressed an interest in receiving help.

Make follow-up contact with parents.

Be sure to give the parent a follow-up call in a few days to let him or her know whether or not the student's behavior at school is improving. If necessary, review the behavior management techniques once more and ask the parent if the implementation of the techniques is clear. If problems are continuing, you may want to use a home-school contract (see Chapter 11).

⌐⌐ Acting now will save time
└┘ and effort in the future.

By helping the parent develop better disciplinary skills at home, you stand a better chance of seeing misbehavior fade at school, now and in the future. After all, it won't help you to enlist the help of a parent who can't carry through. The time spent may well save you hours of disciplinary action in the future.

Helping Parents Support Your Disciplinary Efforts Do's and Don'ts

Do

- Let parents know that, if they agree to it, you will work with them to help solve their child's behavior problems.

- Clearly explain to parents how important it is that they follow through with both disciplinary consequences and positive reinforcement.

- Give parents a tip sheet outlining specific behavior management techniques to use at home.

- Put yourself in the parent's position throughout this conversation. Recognize that it may not be easy to receive advice on handling one's own children. Above all, be sensitive to this issue.

Don't

- Don't give parents behavior management advice unless you know they want your suggestions.

- Don't work with parents on your own if you suspect the child has emotional problems. Involve the psychologist, counselor or administrator in any efforts you make.

✔ Helping Parents Support Your Disciplinary Efforts Checklist

Refer to this checklist each time you plan to advise a parent on behavior management techniques to use at home.

Have you:

_____ Made sure that the parent wants your advice on disciplining his or her child?

_____ Determined to the best of your ability that the child or parent does not have emotional problems that should be dealt with by a counselor?

_____ Reviewed the guidelines for using the five techniques presented in this chapter?

_____ Made copies of the Discipline Sheets for Parents to give to parents?

Regularly Scheduled
Parent Conferences

66 . . .lay a foundation for future positive
parent involvement. **99**

Successful parent conferences are an essential part of getting and
keeping parent support. A regularly scheduled conference can be
a pleasant, informative and productive meeting for both parent and
teacher—an opportunity to get to know one another and interact on
behalf of the student.

A regularly scheduled conference isn't the time to surprise parents with negative information about their child's behavior or performance in school. These problems should never be saved for routine conferences. They need to be dealt with as soon as they occur (refer to Chapters 9 and 10).

Preparing for the Conference

As with all parent contacts, planning is the difference between a mediocre, lackluster meeting and a motivating, successful conference. The confidence you need to project at a conference is the result of careful planning. Follow each of the following steps and ensure a more productive conference for everyone.

1. Send home a conference invitation.

2. Plan the physical environment of your classroom.

3. Put together samples of each student's work.

4. Fill out a Parent Conference Form for each student.

Step 1: Send home a conference invitation.

Your invitation should be warm and friendly, but it must be informative as well. You will be supplying the parent with information *and* asking for some in return. This way, you will both approach the conference better prepared and better informed.

Include the following information in your invitation:

- **Explain the purpose of having a parent conference.**
Parents may not even know why they are being asked to come to a school conference. They may think a) it's to hear bad news about their child or b) the conference is really a waste of their time. You need to let them know why you hold parent conferences and what you hope to accomplish. Stress the importance of the parent being there. Inform parents that you are holding conferences for the parents of all students.

For example:

> On November 11, 12, and 13 I will be holding conferences for the parents of all of my students. This conference is a very important part of the school year. It is our opportunity to get to know each other better and plan how we will work together for your child's benefit."

- **Offer parents flexible time choices.**

A majority of parents work outside the home and can't always come to school in the middle of the day. It is extremely important that you recognize this fact and act accordingly. Few situations are as unsettling to a parent as feeling prevented from participating in their child's education—especially when they want to be included. Whenever possible, set up conference times early in the morning, late in the afternoon, or in the evening. It may not be as convenient for you, but parents will appreciate your willingness to recognize the realities of their lives.

Give parents as much choice as possible in choosing the day of the week and the time for the conference. Your invitation might include a portion that is returned to you indicating when the parent can attend. (Suggestion: Some teachers circulate a parent-conference-time schedule at Back-to-School Night. The schedule lists all dates and times available for conferences. Parents sign their names on the dates and times desired. As conference time approaches, reminders are sent home to parents.)

Give parents as much choice as possible in choosing the day of the week and the time for the conference.

- **Ask parents to let you know what they would like to discuss.**

Include a section on the invitation for the parent to list any issues he or she would like to discuss at the conference. This gives a parent the opportunity to think in advance about what he or she would like to talk about. And having this information ahead of time will better prepare you to address their concerns.

- **Write a personal comment on the invitation.**

Whenever you personalize a reproduced letter that goes home, you are showing parents that you've put in just a bit more effort and care. Take a minute or two to jot down a friendly "I'm looking forward to talking with you" on the parent conference invitation. And be sure to sign your name. Parents will notice these personal touches.

Here's an example of a parent conference invitation:

Dear Parent(s)

During the week of November 14-18 I will be holding conferences with the parents of all my students. I am looking forward to this opportunity for you and me to talk about your child's educational experiences this year. We have an important job to do—to make this a productive, happy year for your child. At the conference we will discuss your child's progress in school, my goals for the remainder of the year and any other issues that affect you or your child. I am certain that this meeting will be productive for all of us! Working together we can make this the best year ever for your child.

Sincerely,

Mr. Ryan

(continues)

Please take a few moments to fill out the lower portion of this letter. When completed, send it back to school.

- -

Parent's name _____

Student's name _____

Please check off your first and second choices of the dates and times most convenient for you. I will do my best to set our meeting for your first-choice time.

These are the dates I prefer:

☐ Monday, November 14
☐ Tuesday, November 15
☐ Wednesday, November 16
☐ Thursday, November 17
☐ Friday, November 18

These are the times I prefer:

Morning: ☐ 6:30 ☐ 7:00 ☐ 7:30 ☐ 8:00
Afternoon: ☐ 3:00 ☐ 3:30 ☐ 4:00 ☐ 4:30 ☐ 5:00
Evening   ☐ 6:30 ☐ 7:00 ☐ 7:30 ☐ 8:00 ☐ 8:30

Do you have any concerns or questions you'd like to discuss with me at the conference? Please write them down below. It's important that we have the opportunity to talk about the issues that are important to you.

Sample parent conference invitation

Step 2: Plan the physical environment.

It's difficult to feel professional (or be perceived as such) when you are sitting face to face with a parent who is stuffed behind a primary desk or perched precariously on an undersized chair. Make sure parents are comfortable during the conference. Arrange to have adult-sized chairs in your room.

If possible, set up a coffee maker and offer coffee and/or tea. Make a positive impression before the conference begins by giving some thought to the comfort of parents as they wait their turn. Place two chairs outside the door along with a stack of student textbooks and workbooks for parents to look at.

Step 3: Put together samples of each student's classwork.

Have examples of the student's classwork available for the conference. Use the work to help you illustrate statements you are making to the parents regarding the student's performance in class.

Step 4: Fill out a Parent Conference Form for each student before meeting the parent(s).

A parent conference must be tightly structured. You have only a limited amount of time, and much to discuss. Prepare yourself by writing down all of the issues you wish to discuss with a parent. Knowing in advance what you are going to talk about can save you from inadvertently leaving out important points. If you are prepared, you'll be more relaxed. And when you are relaxed, your confidence will show and the parent will, in turn, feel more confidence in you.

Here's an example of a well-structured planning sheet. Each of the points listed should be addressed when you meet with parents. Notice that three of the points are to be filled in during the conference with parent comments. On pages 198-201 we'll take a detailed look at each point and examine how it would be approached in the conference.

Parent Conference Planning and Note Sheet

Student's name_____ Time_____
Parent's name_____ Date_____

1. Example of student's unique quality.

2. Past problems to be updated at the conference.

3. Academic strengths of the student.

4. Academic weaknesses that should be discussed.

5. Academic goals for the student for the rest of the year.

6. Parent input on student's academic performance.

7. Social strengths of the student.

8. Weaknesses in the area of social development.

9. Social development goals for the rest of the year.

10. Parent input regarding student's social behavior.

11. Additional issues parent wishes to discuss.

*Sample
parent conference
planning and note
sheet*

Now let's take a detailed look at each point listed on the planning sheet and how it would be approached in the conference.

1. Begin by sharing an example of the unique qualities of their child.

Parents come to conferences to learn about their child's progress. They also want to be satisfied that the teacher understands and appreciates the unique qualities of their child. It is important that you show parents that you've taken the time and interest to get to know their child.

For example:

> *"Yuki has such a great sense of humor. Let me tell you a joke she told last week—she had the entire class laughing!"*

> *"Leon is such a warm and caring child. Just yesterday he helped a younger student who had fallen on the playground."*

> *"Kara has a real passion for art. It is a pleasure to watch her when she is involved in painting."*

> *"Mayra is a leader among her classmates. Let me tell you how she handled a tough situation between several students."*

2. Give an update on any past problems.

If you have dealt with the parent about a problem in the past, make sure you spend some time updating the current status of the situation. It's important to attend to this as soon as possible because the parent will most likely be anxious about it and that anxiety may keep him or her from listening to anything else you discuss.

> *"I'm happy to tell you that Erin is turning in all of her homework assignments now."*

> *"Felipe is doing much better controlling his temper. I can see the effort he's making. You should be very proud of him."*

> *"Math continues to be a problem for Bob, but during this*

Parents On Your Side

*conference I'm going to give you some specific guide-
lines for helping him at home."*

3. Discuss academic strengths.

Focus on the positive academic strengths of the student. Show
examples of classwork at this time. If appropriate, you may wish to
use the student's report card as a guide for this discussion.

*"You can see from these papers that Kelly's writing skills
have steadily improved this year. Her use of vocabulary
is much more descriptive than it was in October."*

*"Here's where Jaime was at the start of the year in
reading. Now look at this. He's moved ahead three
levels. You can see from these tests that his comprehension skills are excellent."*

*"Troy did a great job organizing and writing this term
paper. His research was thorough, his note cards well
written, and the final paper was carefully thought out and
interesting to read. You should be very proud of him."*

4. If appropriate, discuss academic weaknesses.

If the child is having academic problems, let the parent know you are
taking steps to improve the situation.

*"I'm aware, of course, that Kenneth is struggling to keep
up in Spanish. I have some lessons on tape that I think will
help him. I'd like to send them home with you. Here's
how to use them . . ."*

*"Algebra 1 is very difficult for Michael. I've arranged to
have him work with a senior tutor two days a week
during classtime."*

5. Get parental input on the child's academic performance.

Ask parents how they feel their child is doing in school. It is important
that parents have the opportunity to give feedback. If they feel there's
a problem that you are overlooking you need to address the issue
and clear up any misunderstanding. Ask questions such as:

*"Are you satisfied with your child's academic perform-
ance?"*

"Do you have any concerns about how your child is doing in school?"

Take notes on what the parent says.

6. Discuss academic goals for the remainder of the year.

Talk to the parent about what you'd like to see the child accomplish the rest of the year. Get the parent's input, too. Knowing that both of you have the same goals will help establish a rapport that may be needed if difficulties arise later.

"By the end of the year, Jackie should know his multiplication tables through 12."

"I would like to see Sara reading at grade level by June. Considering how well she's doing now, I think we will meet this goal."

"Rebecca's research skills should improve considerably over the next few months. We will be doing some assignments geared toward this goal."

7. Present the social strengths of the student.

Discuss the student's social behavior in your class by focusing on his or her strengths in relating to peers. Be prepared to give specific examples.

"Larry is always there to help out a friend. His loyalty is really valued by the other students. They know they can count on him."

"Rosa's exuberance and spirit make her someone that students and teachers enjoy being with."

8. If appropriate, discuss the student's weaknesses in social interactions.

Be sensitive. Link any suggestions or observations you have to a positive statement or observation.

"I'd like to see Ben feel more confident about himself when he's in a group. He's a smart boy, but I'm not so sure he thinks so."

"As you are aware, Paul too often lets anger control him. I think, however, that the behavior contract you are using at home and I'm using at school is making a difference."

9. Discuss your goals in the area of social development for the remainder of the school year.

"I would like to see Kathryn become a bit more assertive in class. I know she has opinions she'd like to offer, but she holds back. I'm going to have the students do some cooperative learning activities. The small-group setting should help Kathryn overcome some of her hesitance."

10. Get parental input regarding the child's social behavior.
Ask the parent how they perceive their child is doing socially:

"Do you feel your child is happy in school?"

"Does your child play with friends outside of school?"

"What are your concerns regarding your child's relationships with other students?"

11. Finally, talk about any other issues parents may wish to discuss.
Ask if there's anything else the parent would like to talk about with you. At this time you should also address any issues that the parent wrote about on the conference notification.

Conducting the Conference

Set a professional, caring tone.
The attitude you project at the conference is what will ultimately win a parent's confidence, trust and support. Keep the "golden rule" of parent communication in mind at all times: Treat parents the way you would wanted to be treated. At a conference, the parent is your guest in the classroom. You are the host and it's your responsibility to see that it is a pleasurable, productive and informative experience.

Greet the parent warmly and enthusiastically.
First impressions do count. Whether it's 6:30 in the morning or 7:30 at night, wake up, put on a smile and make the parent feel welcome.

Greet the parent at the door, give a firm handshake and usher him or her to a seat. Offer coffee or tea and spend a moment or two putting the parent at ease.

Refer to your Parent Conference Form as you proceed through the conference.

Your planning sheet helped you focus on your goals as you planned for the meeting. Be sure you use this valuable resource during the conference, too. Keep it in front of you as you speak and jot down points of interest as they come up.

Use effective listening and communication skills.

The way you speak and listen to a parent can have great impact in enhancing that parent's trust and confidence in what you are saying. Be sensitive to the parent, treating him or her the way you would want to be treated if your own child were the object of the conversation. With this in mind, be on the lookout for any roadblocks that may appear, and use your communication skills to move the parent past the roadblock. This conference is a good opportunity for you to interact with parents in a positive, supportive atmosphere. Make the most of it. If a parent seems overwhelmed, hostile, negative or confused, don't ignore it, remedy it. Your confident, professional attitude and appropriate responses can turn an uninvolved parent into a supportive one. (See pages 158-160 for a review of effective listening skills.)

Close the conference on a positive, optimistic note.

At the close of the conference, rise, shake the parent's hand and walk together to the door. Make sure your parting comments are sincere. Leave the parent with a positive, confident feeling that he or she has just met with an educator who really cares, and who will be there for the child all year long.

> *"I'm so glad we've had this conference, Mr. Peterson. I think the goals we both have for your son are clear. And now that we know each other better, I'm sure we can work together to make this year a real success for Rob. I look forward to speaking to you again soon."*

Ⓓ Regularly Scheduled Parent Conference Do's and Don'ts

Do

- Arrive at the conference site before the parent.

- Greet the parent warmly.

- Usher the parent to the seat you've selected.

- Look the parent in the eyes when speaking.

- Address the parent often by name.

- Say something complimentary about the student early in the conference.

- Hand the parent the child's work to look over. Point out examples of work that should be noted.

- Have study or academic tips available to give to parents.

- Ask the parent for his or her input regarding the student.

- End the conference on time, and schedule another one if needed.

- Make detailed notes of what was discussed.

Don't

- Don't surprise parents with new problems. Parents should be notified the moment a problem arises.

- Don't make small talk. Use every moment of the parent's time to discuss the student's progress.

- Don't discuss other students, even if the parent tries to.

- Don't do all the talking. You want to maintain control of the conference, but you should allow the parent time to discuss his or her concerns and ideas. You may learn something important that can help you in dealing with the child.

☑ Regularly Scheduled Parent Conference Checklist

Refer to this checklist when you plan your parent-teacher conferences.

Have you:

_____ Sent an invitation that explains why a parent should attend the conference?

_____ Made flexible time choices available to parents?

_____ Asked parents to let you know what they would like to discuss?

_____ Organized samples of each student's classwork?

_____ Planned where parents will sit for the conference? Arranged for coffee or tea?

_____ Filled out a Parent Conference Form for each student?

_____ Collected appropriate study or academic tips to give parents so that they can help their child at home?

Chapter 14
Difficult Situations

> 66 ...*when they occur, you have to be prepared to stand your ground and respond with confidence.* 99

If you haven't already, sooner or later you will encounter parents who make things difficult for you. They may be angry at you or angry at the school. They may be upset by years of perceived (or real) injustices. They may be frustrated by their inability to deal with their children, or they may just be overwhelmed by the stress in their own lives. Whatever the reason, these are parents whose roadblocks threaten to undermine your teaching efforts.

At first, these roadblocks may seem unsurmountable They may appear to be so established that you're sure you've come to a dead end with this parent. Not true. You may be detoured, but you *can* get back on track.

Throughout this book we have stressed the importance of developing an effective attitude, and of holding fast to professionalism and confidence. We have reiterated the importance of listening for roadblocks—your own as well as those of parents. As we have seen, effective teachers are those who have the ability to deal with problems as they appear.

Effective teachers are those who have the ability to deal with problems as they appear.

Now is when you will really see the benefits of what you've learned in *Parents On Your Side*. When you know that you can deal effectively with the most difficult situations, you will know you have learned your techniques well.

Preparation Is the Key.

"This parent came in and just read me the riot act. I had lowered her daughter's grade on a term paper because it was turned in late. But according to the parent, I was to blame. She said I was such a lousy teacher that her daughter didn't know how to do the work. I didn't know how to respond. I was just shaking. And the worse part of it was that all of my students were watching!"

You can't avoid situations like these. You can't even anticipate them. When they occur you have to be prepared to stand your ground and proceed with confidence. You have a lot riding on this moment, and you need to handle it carefully, professionally and effectively. The well-being of your students depends upon your ability to reach the parent then and there.

As you've probably told your students, the more thoroughly you learn your lessons, the easier they will be to apply. Those same words pertain to you here. When a difficult situation arises, you won't have time to check in this book for the right technique or the most effective phrases to use. You must have already learned the words, the attitude and the techniques and made them part of your teaching style.

Here then are some specialized communication skills that will help you handle challenging situations. Learn them now, before you need them.

Communication skills for difficult situations:

• How to disarm criticism.

• How to keep a conference focused on *your* goals.

• How to get a commitment from non-cooperative parents.

• How to handle a parent who makes an unscheduled visit to school.

• How to handle phone calls from parents.

How to Disarm Criticism

"I do the best job I can for my students. So it's always hard when a parent criticizes my teaching or accuses me of not caring about their child. It hurts. All I can think about is defending myself."

One of the most distressing situations you encounter as a teacher is to be on the receiving end of a barrage of criticism by a parent. It's usually unanticipated, generally uncomfortable and almost always hurtful.

"You're the cause of my daughter's problem."

"If you knew what you were doing, my son wouldn't be in this mess."

"Your assignments are boring. Why would she want to study?"

"My son's never had problems before, so you must be doing something wrong."

Though comments like these may sting at first, don't become hurt or angry. Stay in control. Recognize that you're dealing with a very distraught parent and that you've got to keep a clear head. Maintain a professional attitude. *Don't* react in this way:

> *"Look, I'm doing the best job I can."*
>
> *"I have 149 other students. I can't spend all of my time with your child."*
>
> *"I've tried everything. You just don't realize how hard it is dealing with your child."*

Reactionary statements like these are not the words of a confident professional. They inspire neither respect nor understanding from the parent. Defensive responses such as these will not help you break down a parent's anger. They only shut down communication and leave the parent no choice but to continue his or her criticism. And once this cycle begins, it's hard to break.

You need to know how to quickly disarm the criticism and get the parent back on a more productive track.

Follow these guidelines:

If the parent's concern and criticism are justified, accept your mistake.

Sometimes parents are justified in their criticism. Teachers, like anyone else, can make a mistake. It's difficult, however, in the face of an angry tirade, to sit back and think, "Wait a minute, maybe there's some truth to what this parent is saying." You have to take this step, though, if you are to turn a confrontation into a more positive relationship. Stop, think, and then answer the parent honestly and straightforwardly. Don't make excuses or place blame on others. Make your statement clearly.

Don't make excuses or place blame on others.

> *"You have reason to be angry. I should have contacted you sooner about this problem."*

"I feel you are right to be upset. I should not have become so upset with your son the other day."

"You have reason to be frustrated. I was unaware that your child had a problem with this subject, and I should have been."

Admitting your mistakes may make you feel uneasy, but just think about the effect your words can have on the parent. Your response may diffuse the parent's pent-up anger and resentment and pave the way for further constructive communication.

If the criticism is incorrect, or only partially correct, follow these steps:

1. Listen to the parent's complaints without defending or justifying yourself.
The parent is angry and needs to talk. Give him or her the chance to "let it out." Use your effective listening skills (see pages 158-160). Look at the parent while he or she is speaking and make it clear that you are paying attention to what is being said. Let the parent vent his or her anger or frustration.

2. Show your empathy and concern by asking the parent for more specific information about the complaint.
This is the most useful way to disarm a parent's criticism. By asking questions, you are showing that you care about what the parent is saying. In addition, you are showing that you are able to handle criticism and maintain control in the conversation.

"That really concerns me. Can you explain more about what you mean?"

"Can you give me some examples of what you are saying?"

"Have I done something like this before?"

Remember, justified or not, the parent's anger is real. People who are angry need to feel they are being listened to. Let the parent talk it out.

3. Now, refocus the conversation. Restate the student's problem behavior and clarify why it is not in his or her best interests to act this way.

After listening, you must refocus the conversation on the child's behavior and move away from the parent's criticism.

> *"I understand how upset you are, but we still must help your child get his work done so he won't fall behind."*

> *"I hear your point, but your daughter must do her homework or her grades will drop."*

> *"I really hear what your are saying, but we must help your son stop his disruptive behavior in class so he does not continue to get into trouble."*

4. If a parent is still critical or angry, point out that conflict between the two of you is harmful to the student.

Be a peacemaker. Explain that continued antagonism is not in anyone's best interests, especially the child's.

> *"I hear your point, but our disagreeing will only harm Stuart and will not help him solve his problem."*

> *"You have a right to be upset with me, but this won't help Tom."*

> *"I know we don't see eye-to-eye on this issue, but we are not going to help Julie if we don't work together."*

5. Finally, if the parent is still upset, suggest that he or she talks with the principal.

Do not allow a critical parent to continue criticizing you. If it becomes clear that the parent is not going to calm down, it is appropriate to have the parent talk to the principal. Just bringing up this alternative may calm the parent down.

> *"It seems as though you and I cannot resolve this issue, so maybe you should speak with the principal about it."*

Here is a sample dialogue of a teacher using the techniques described to disarm a parent's criticism.

Teacher: I'm concerned about Ted's fighting. He's had three fights with other students in the last three days.

Parent: He says the other kids pick on him and you don't do anything about it.

Teacher: *(listening, nodding head)* Uh huh.

Parent: It's just not right. He's never had problems in school before. I just don't know what's going on in your room.

Teacher: *(asking for more information)* Can you tell me more of what he says about how the kids pick on him?

Parent: He says Bob and Kevin tease him. He says sometimes you're standing right there and you don't do anything.

Teacher: Are there any other problems he's had with students that he's told you about where he felt I did nothing?

Parent: He said the same thing happened last week with Jeremy.

Teacher: Mrs. Cole, I can understand why you would be upset if you were told he was being picked on and I watched and did nothing. I do not allow students to pick on one another. I would never condone this behavior by ignoring it. But we really have to discuss ways to help Ted stop fighting. We both want what's best for him, and if we work together we can have that.

How to Keep a Conference Focused on Your Goals

"I feel as though I'm prepared when I begin a confer-
ence, but with some parents it just seems to fall apart.
Usually these are parents who have something to com-
plain about. When the conference is over, they've said
it all and I'm left thinking about what I didn't get a chance
to say."

Too often, teachers lose control of a conference because the parent takes over the agenda. Staying in control of a conference means keeping parents focused on your goals. This can be difficult when parents are upset or anxious. They may want to talk about other problems the student is having, problems they are having at home, or excuses for why the student is behaving this way. When teachers get sidetracked and allow the parent's goals to divert the conference in a non-productive direction, little is accomplished.

We will look at two very effective techniques for keeping a conference focused on your objectives. These techniques, the Broken-Record and the Wrong-Person techniques, are very effective for keeping a conference in focus. The Broken-Record technique and the Wrong-Person technique can be used in a variety of situations which demand that attention be paid to the issue at hand.

Stay focused. Use the Broken-Record technique.
You can keep from getting sidetracked by using the Broken-Record technique. When you use the Broken Record, you keep repeating your goals for the conference again and again, like a broken record.

Here's how to use this technique:

Clearly communicate to the parent that you understand his or her
concerns and goals. Then restate your goal for the conference.

Parent: I wish somebody at this school would do something about the way the other kids are acting on the yard. Every day, Ron comes home telling me about how all the kids are getting him mad and making him get into fights.

| Teacher: | Mrs. Evans, I understand you feel the other children are picking on your son *(indicate that you understand the parent's concern)*, but we need to focus on how we can work together to help your son stop fighting at school *(restatement of goal)*. |

If the parent continues to focus on different goals, or argues with you, keep repeating your goal without being sidetracked by the parent's comments.

| Parent: | But he comes home every day upset about what the other kids say. I want something to be done about this. |

| Teacher: | I understand your concern about your child being picked on, but **we must focus on how we can stop him from fighting in school** *(Broken Record)*. |

| Parent: | But he always says it's not his fault. Like I've told you, the kids won't leave him alone. |

| Teacher: | At a later time we can discuss the children picking on your son. I understand how concerned you are about that. But our time here today is limited, and **we must discuss how we can help him stop fighting in school** *(Broken Record)*. |

When you use the Broken Record, you are showing the parent that you recognize his/her concern, but that you also have enough control and confidence to redirect the conference back to the problem at hand.

NOTE: Be sure to use the Broken Record only when the parent is trying to divert you in a manipulative way. If the parent brings up a legitimate concern that is vital to the solution of the problem, don't use the Broken Record to cut off communication.

The Wrong-Person Technique

Some parents will try to shift the responsibility for their child's poor behavior onto a teacher's shoulders. They will make it seem as though you, rather than the student, are the one causing the problem. The Wrong-Person technique can help the parent focus on the real situation. When using this technique, take care not to sound hostile or as if you are putting the parent down. Keep your mind on the golden rule and speak to the parent in the manner in which you would like to be spoken if the situation were reversed.

Teacher: If Evan chooses to continue to misbehave, I will be forced to keep him after school.

Parent: Wait just a minute. You can't do that. If you keep him after school, he'll miss the bus. Then I'll have to leave work to pick him up. If I don't work, I don't get paid.

Teacher: Mr. Curtis, I think you're talking to the wrong person. If you don't want to miss work, you'll have to talk to Evan about that.

Teacher:	Kristin broke a class rule three times today. That means she will have to stay fifteen minutes after school tomorrow.
Parent:	I'm sorry, but you can't have Kristin stay late tomorrow. She has soccer practice.
Teacher:	Mrs. Kelly, I think you're talking to the wrong person. If Kristin does not want to stay after school, she will have to learn to follow the school rules.

How to Get a Commitment from Non-Cooperative Parents

Getting support from a non-cooperative parent may depend on more than disarming criticism or keeping the conversation focused. At some point, you will have to get a commitment from the parent to support you. This can be difficult, especially when the parent is still angry, upset or overwhelmed.

There are specific steps you can take to motivate these parents to support you. You need to let parents know:

• why it is in their child's best interest that they support you.

• why you, as a teacher, cannot handle a problem on your own.

• what the outcome will be for the child if the parent does not work with you.

Here's what to do:

Emphasize that you cannot solve their child's problem on your own.
You must clearly explain to the parent that you are limited in your ability to motivate their child to improve behavior or classroom performance. Parents must understand that the greatest power to affect change lies with them.

> ❝ I want to be very clear with you. As a teacher, there is only so much I can do to motivate your child to behave at school. I can promise you that I will do everything in my

power to help your child. But you must understand that you are really the one(s) who can make the difference.

Point out that the parent is the most influential person in a child's life.

Stress to parents that they are truly the most important persons in their child's life.

 You are the most important person in your child's life. What you say to your child, and what you expect of him, make a tremendous difference in how he looks at himself. You have the ability to turn things around for your child. But to do that, you must be willing to support my efforts here at school.

Present the negative outcome you feel will occur if the parent does not support you.

Sometimes you have to lay it on the line. A parent who won't get involved is jeopardizing his or her child's success in school—and needs to know what that can mean. Too often teachers avoid letting a parent know the potential consequences of their non-involvement.

Here are some typical problems students have, and the potential short-term and long-term negative outcomes:

> **Problem:** The student will not do homework.
>
> <u>Short-term negative outcomes:</u>
> The student will fall behind in class.
> The student will fail tests.
> The student will earn poor grades.
>
> <u>Long-term negative outcomes:</u>
> The student may be held back in school.
> The student will never reach academic potential.
> The student has greater potential of dropping out of school.

Problem: The student fights with peers.

Short-term negative outcomes:

The student will continue to receive detention at school.

The student will have fewer and fewer friends.

The student will face suspension.

Long-term negative outcomes:

The student's self-esteem decreases.

The student will never learn to deal appropriately with conflict.

The student will face the real possibility of expulsion when her or she is older.

The student will not get along with co-workers as as an adult.

Problem: The student is chronically tardy or truant.

Short-term negative outcomes:

The student will fall behind academically.

The student may eventually be suspended.

Long-term negative outcomes:

The student may be held back.

The student may eventually drop out of school.

If necessary, here's what to say to parents:

It's my responsibility to tell you what you can expect to happen if you don't support my efforts to help your child. Your child is not turning in any homework assignments or classroom assignments at all. And because he's not doing his work, he's not keeping up in class and he's failing his tests. Unless the situation changes, he will fail this subject. And that means a strong possibility of being held back next year. Mrs. Rey, those are just the short-term consequences he faces. I must also tell you that students who are held back for these reasons run a much greater risk of ultimately dropping out of school. And the long-term consequences of that are loss of self-esteem, poorer choices of jobs, and a life that just isn't as full of promise as it could have been."

How to Deal with a Parent Who Makes an Unscheduled Visit to School

"I was standing in front of the class giving a social studies lecture when this parent roared through the door demanding that I talk to him right then and there. He was obviously ready to explode. I wasn't sure what to do."

Few incidents are as upsetting as having a parent barge into your classroom or stop you in the hall on the way to class demanding to discuss an issue with you—on the spot. You are caught off guard, students are present and the parent may be angry and impatient. This is a situation that you must handle skillfully, or it can become extremely unpleasant for you, the parent and the student(s).

Here are some very simple techniques to use when handling these difficult situations:

First, be sensitive to the parent's concerns.

Keep this in mind: No matter how inappropriately a parent is behaving, he or she obviously must be upset or anxious to have to come to school in this manner. If at all possible, stop what you are doing and listen. Put yourself in the parent's place. Be sensitive to what he or she is saying.

"Mrs. Santiago, you must be very upset to come here today to talk to me."

"Mr. Burke, I can see that you are very worried about Tracy's grades or you wouldn't be coming to school like this."

Let the parent know that his or her concerns are too important to discuss at this time.

Diffuse the parent's anger. Let him or her know that you, too, want to discuss the problem, but that you would prefer to schedule a meeting at a time that is more conducive to finding a solution.

"I hear how upset you are about Paul's suspension. This issue is too important to discuss now when I've got

twenty-five students here. We need to find a time when we can discuss it in more detail."

"I hear how upset you are with how I dealt with your son. This is too important to discuss now when I have to be in class in two minutes. We need to find a time when we can meet and talk."

Set a time with the parent to talk about the problem.
Be very careful not to let the parent feel you're putting him or her off. Assure the parent that you want to discuss the issue further. Tell the parent exactly when he or she can expect to hear from you.

"I will call you as soon as school is over today and we can discuss it further."

"Could you please wait for me in the office? I have a break in fifteen minutes. I'd like to talk to you about setting a time when we can meet."

"I will call you at home tonight. We'll make an appointment to get together and discuss this problem."

If necessary, get administrative help.
If the previously mentioned techniques do not work, and the parent stays in the classroom or continues to follow you through the halls, get help from the principal or vice principal immediately. If necessary, give a note to a student to take to the office asking for assistance. This is especially important if a parent is out of control and making threats. Under no circumstances should you stand there and allow a parent to verbally abuse or threaten you.

If necessary, get administrative help.

Here's an example of a teacher dealing effectively with an angry parent who's made an unscheduled visit to school:

The teacher is walking in the hall on her way to class.

Parent: Mrs. Shelby, I want to speak with you right now. How in the (blank) can you suspend my daughter? What is your problem?

Teacher: Mrs. Webster, can you explain what you mean?

Parent: Yes, I can explain what I mean. You sent Denise home. I had to leave work. I really can't believe this. You are on my kid's case every single day. I've had it with you and this school.

Teacher: I hear how angry and upset you are.

Parent: You're right about that. I've had it.

Teacher: Mrs. Webster, this issue is too important for us to discuss now. I'm on my way to class. I want to talk to you about this in greater detail, but we'll have to talk later.

Parent: I want to talk about it now.

Teacher: I understand, Mrs. Webster, but this is much too important for us to discuss now. I will call you as soon as school is out today at 3:30. Will you be home?

Parent: Well, I won't be home. I have to go to work and make up the time I've lost because you suspended Denise.

Teacher: Then can I call you at work?

Parent: No, you know you can't call me at work. I'm in enough trouble there already.

Teacher:	Then what time do you get home from work?
Parent:	About 7:00.
Teacher:	Then I'll call your home tonight at 7:30.
Parent:	You'd better do that!
Teacher:	I promise I will call you at 7:30 tonight. I hear how upset you are and I want to help Denise as much as you do.

How to Handle Phone Calls from Parents

"It's one thing for me to make the phone call to a parent. I can prepare myself and take charge of the conversation. It's a lot harder when I get a message that a parent wants me to call him. I may not know what the parent is concerned or upset about. I have to be ready for anything."

In Chapter 7 you learned how to structure a conversation when you call a parent about a problem. But what happens when the parent calls you? Obviously, you can't plan exactly what you will say. Every phone call from a parent is different. You can, however, be prepared to handle the parent's emotional state as well as taking steps toward solving the problem.

Here are some guidelines to follow:

1. Listen to what the parent has to say.

If a parent calls you, he or she is concerned about something. At the beginning of the conversation, just listen to what the parent has to say. Don't interrupt or try to cut the parent's comments short. Listen carefully and take notes.

2. Be sensitive to the parent's concerns.

You may feel the parent is overreacting to something. You may feel he or she is being overly protective. You may even feel the parent is being manipulated by the child. That doesn't matter. What does matter is that you make sure that anything you say reflects an awareness that the parent is upset or concerned about this issue. Under no circumstances should you make value judgements, for example, "It's ridiculous for you to be upset," or "There's no reason for you to be concerned." Comments like these will alienate the parent and hinder further productive conversation.

Make sure that anything you say reflects an awareness that the parent is upset or concerned about this issue.

3. Use "disarming criticism" techniques if necessary.

Review the techniques found on pages 207-211 of this chapter. These techniques can be used just as effectively in a phone conversation as in a face-to-face conference. Listen to the parent's concerns, ask for more information and be empathetic to his or her feelings. Under no circumstances should you become defensive, try to blame the student or tell the parent he or she is wrong in calling. Handle the situation well and you may open the door to future positive communication with this parent.

4. If you did something wrong, apologize.

If the parent has a legitimate concern, apologize.

If the parent has a legitimate concern, the best technique is to simply apologize for making a mistake. Don't become defensive. Don't minimize your actions. Apologize clearly to the parent and reassure him or her that such actions will not occur again. (See pages 208-209 for more details.)

5. If the parent is misinformed, point out the facts.

Sometimes a parent may call because of something the child says is going on in your classroom. The student's reporting may be inaccurate, but it is still very important that you listen to the parent's concerns before gently but firmly pointing out the truth.

"Mrs. Debs, I understand that Cleavon told you he has been given five worksheets to do in ten minutes and that there's no way he can finish them on time. The truth is, Mrs. Debs, that he, and the other students, have been given two worksheets that can easily be done in the time allowed if the students stick to their work."

"Mr. Landry, I understand that Benjamin said he was singled out and embarrassed in front of the whole class. I understand that he may feel that way, but here is what happened. He was shouting in class. I walked over to him and, very quietly and privately, told him that he had a choice to either stop shouting or sit away from the other children. He continued to shout and so he was told to sit in the time-out spot."

6. Do not make quick decisions.

When a parent is upset, he or she is likely to want you to make a quick decision to change something: your discipline methods, your teaching methods, your curriculum, your classroom organization, etc. Unless you agree that the particular situation warrants immediate action, do not allow the parent to pressure you into making changes before you've carefully thought them through. Let the parent know you hear what he or she is saying and you understand the concern, but that you want to think about the situation before taking any action.

"Mrs. Rogers, I hear what you are saying about changing Stephanie's reading group. I want to give this situation some thought. I will call you tomorrow to discuss it further."

"Mr. Hill, I understand you want Greg's seat changed. There's some merit to what you are saying. I want to think

about the affect it would have on him and I will talk to you about it tomorrow."

7. If appropriate, ask the parent to come in for a conference.

If a parent raises an issue that cannot be easily resolved in a brief phone conversation, ask him or her to come in for a conference to discuss it further. This will communicate to the parent your concern and interest in what he or she has to say.

8. Admit you do not have all the answers.

If the parent raises an issue regarding a student's academic performance or behavior that you do not have an answer for, do not hesitate to say so. You don't have to pretend to know everything. However, you should reassure the parent that you understand his or her concern and will look into the matter further. For example:

You don't have to pretend to know everything.

"I hear what you are saying. I do not have an answer, but I will meet with the (principal/psychologist/counselor) and I will contact you again with some information that can help your daughter."

"I hear what you are saying. I do not have an answer, but I will speak with the director of the after-school care program and get back to you with some ideas for helping your son."

9. Thank the parent for calling.

Whatever the nature of the conversation, let the parent know that you appreciate the fact that he or she called. Try to end the conversation on as positive a note as possible.

"Thank you for calling this to my attention. I will look into it and call you with a response tomorrow."

"I understand that this is a difficult situation. I appreciate your telling me your feelings about it.

■■ Techniques to Use with the ■■ Most Difficult Parents

"I have one parent this year that I can't seem to reach— no matter what I do. She avoids me, won't answer my calls, and when I do get hold of her she makes it clear that she wants nothing to do with me or the school. Unfortunately, her son is on his way to losing it all. I can't let that happen. Not until I've tried everything I possibly can."

Then there's the one parent you can't seem to reach, no matter what you do.

The ideas, suggestions and techniques presented in *Parents On Your Side* will enable you to get 98% of parents on your side. The remaining 2% are the hardest of all to handle. You may need to employ additional techniques if you are to have any chance of successfully reaching these parents.

NOTE: The methods presented in this chapter should only be used with administrative support.

Method 1- Take the child home or to the parent's place of work.

If calling the parent doesn't produce results, try doing what the principal did in the following situation:

> George Cotter was the classic fifth-grade troublemaker. He had been a problem since he had transferred to the school at the beginning of the year. His father refused to cooperate when contacted by George's teacher.
>
> One day George threw a chair across the room and missed hitting the head of a fellow student by three inches. The principal, Mrs. Burns, was notified. George was removed from class and suspension proceedings began. The principal phoned Mr. Cotter at work. She spoke first to his supervisor who said Mr. Cotter couldn't come to the phone. Mrs. Burns would not be put off. She told the supervisor that there was an emergency at his son's school. Mr. Cotter came to the phone within two minutes.

Here is the conversation that ensued:

Principal: Mr. Cotter, this is Mrs. Burns, the principal at George's school. Your son was involved in a serious incident today. We need you to come to school immediately and help us work out this problem.

Mr. Cotter: Hey, why are you calling me at work for something like that? I can't come to school now. I've got five more hours on this shift.

Principal: When your son causes problems during our working day, you will have to leave your job and help us solve the problem.

Mr. Cotter: I can't do that. If I leave the factory now, they'll dock my pay.

Principal: Mr. Cotter, you're talking to the wrong person. Every time George chooses to disrupt his class, I'll have to call you and ask you to take him home. If you don't want to be called, I suggest you talk to him about following the rules. He's becoming a serious problem and the school can no longer be responsible for him.

Mr. Cotter: Wait a minute. That kid is your problem from nine to three.

Principal: No, Mr. Cotter. George is your responsibility twenty-four hours a day. You have a choice. Either you come to school now, or I'll be forced to bring George to you.

Mr. Cotter: Very funny. I'm not leaving work, and I don't want you to call me here ever again.

Principal: You leave me no choice. Goodbye, Mr. Cotter.

With that, the principal took care of some last minute details, ushered George to her car and drove to the father's place of employment. It was a long drive, about ten miles away, but Mrs. Burns was determined to solve the problem of George's behavior once and for all.

Mrs. Burns took George into the supervisor's office, explained the situation to him, and Mr. Cotter was summoned. Seeing his son and Mrs. Burns standing next to his angry supervisor was very upsetting to Mr. Cotter. He had no choice. He took his son home and lost a day's pay.

The father in this situation was so greatly inconvenienced that he realized the teacher and principal meant business and he finally agreed to work with the school to change his son's behavior. At a meeting with the parent, teacher and principal, a contract was formulated to improve George's behavior. Mr. Cotter agreed to provide discipline whenever he received notice that his son was disruptive in school. Rewards for good reports were also agreed upon. The principal, teacher, parent and student all signed the contract. In addition, the school arranged for regular meetings between George and the guidance counselor. Within three weeks the problem was solved.

> NOTE: Whenever you need to take severe measures such as this to insure parental support, have the guidance counselor follow up on the home situation. There is always the possibility that the child may be physically mentally abused. Report any suspicion of child abuse to the proper authorities.

Method 2- Have the parent monitor student behavior at school.

Some parents simply will not believe their child is a serious problem at school. Others absolutely refuse to do anything about it. In these cases, offer parents a choice—either they come to school and monitor their child, or the school will have to suspend the child. If the parent agrees, have him or her sit in on every class with the student, including cafeteria and gym. (Note: Use this method with older students only. Younger students may find having mom or dad in class pleasurable.)

Offer parents a choice.

To have its greatest effect, the parent must continue coming to school until the student shows improvement or the parent agrees to help.

This method is successful because

- the parent sees exactly how the student behaves in school.

- the parent is usually inconvenienced and eventually agrees to help.

- the student feels pressure from peers about having his or her parent at school and begins to behave.

Method 3- Detain students after school and have parents sign them out.

A frequently used consequence for students who severely misbehave is to detain them after school. Then, when the detention period ends, the parent is required to come to school to sign the student out. A parent who has to leave work to pick up his or her child may be inconvenienced enough to work with the school to improve the child's behavior. Always give parents twenty-four hours notice before using this method.

Method 4- Have parents escort truant students to school.

If a student is continually truant and the parent has not cooperated in solving the problem, offer a choice. The parent must bring the child to school each morning, sign him or her in, or the child will be suspended.

Method 5- Home Visits

As discussed in Chapter 6, a home visit is an effective positive technique to use with parents. Going to a student's home to deliver good news or get acquainted with parents is one of the best means at your disposal to demonstrate your concern. A home visit is also a powerful technique to use with parents you are having trouble reaching or dealing with. A home visit gives you the opportunity to sit down with a parent in his or her own home and discuss the problem at hand. The visit shows the parent you are concerned enough to go out of your way to solve a problem. The visit shows that you mean business.

Follow these guidelines.

1. Do not arrive at a student's home unannounced. Make every effort to set up an appointment. Ask your administrator for help if you are unable to reach the parent.

2. As with any other conference, be prepared. Write down all points you wish to cover with the parent and bring your notes and documentation with you.

3. Review guidelines for disarming criticism and keeping a conference focused on your goals (pages 207-215).

4. Keep a positive and professional attitude. Listen carefully to the parent's concerns and be sensitive to what he or she says.

5. At the end of the visit, let the parent know that there will be follow-up contact from you. Once having made this effort, you will want to do all you can to keep this parent involved.

⌐ Difficult Situations *Can* Be Handled
⌐ Successfully.

Dealing with difficult parents may be unsettling, but when handled with skill and confidence, you *can* move toward a productive outcome. As was stated at the beginning of this chapter, these situations are the ones that will really test your professionalism and confidence.

Speak and act with confidence.

If you speak and act with confidence, if you've learned to recognize and deal with your own roadblocks, if you've practiced and honed your own listening skills so you can recognize and move parents past their own roadblocks, then you have indeed achieved the ability to handle difficult situations and, in doing so, improve the student's chances for success.

If you are unclear about any of the procedures mentioned in this book, now's the time to review them. Get them clear and working for you now. The key to being prepared is having your skills in place before you really need them.

Chapter 15

End the Year on a Positive Note

> **"** *I like to think that I'm doing all I can do to pass along parents and students who are committed to education.* **"**

Throughout this book we have presented many techniques to help you implement a positive parent involvement plan that will carry you successfully from the first day of school to the last. Now's the time to pull it all together and take those final steps that will put the finishing touches on a noteworthy year. The end of the year is your opportunity to make final, meaningful contact with parents and students.

The words you communicate as the year comes to a close will ensure that your students and their parents move forward with the best possible attitude toward school, education and teachers. You're not just ending one year; you're opening the door for all the years ahead. Keep in mind that the effects of everything you've done this year are cumulative. The roadblocks you've cleared won't be roadblocks to the next teacher. What a step forward that is for everyone.

Make Open House a parent thank-you event.

Just as Back-to-School Night set the stage for a year of dynamic parent involvement, Open House in the spring can serve as a retrospective of all that's been accomplished. Traditionally, Open House is a time for parents to tour the classroom with their children, look at their work, and chat amiably with the teacher and other parents. Now that you have parents on your side, it's time to add a new component: a heartfelt thanks to parents for their support.

Let "Thanks to you, it's been a great year" be your theme. Carry it through on the invitations you send home and signs or banners you place in the classroom. Have students write notes to parents thanking them for all of their help. At Open House, present parents with small thank-you favors:

• Have a basket of apples by the door with a sign that reads: An apple from the teacher to the best team of parents ever!

• Have a friend serve as photographer and take a polaroid of each parent and child. Slip each photo into a construction paper frame that says "Thanks to you it's been a great year."

Above all, make sure every parent leaves with the knowledge that his or her help has been noticed, appreciated and worthwhile.

Send end-of-year notes to students.

"It was twenty-five years ago, but I still remember the note Mr. O'Leary wrote to me. It made me feel terrific. Finally, after all was said and done, I knew he thought well of me, and that meant a lot. As a matter of fact, I still have that note somewhere." — Parent

Your words can have a lasting effect on students of any age. At the end of the year, take the time to give your students the gift of a few thoughtfully chosen sentences.

Don't view this correspondence as a perfunctory duty. Get excited about it! You are launching your students into their future. Fuel their journey with the best, most encouraging words you can. Chances are, if you were able to look ahead 25 years, you'd find some of your messages tucked away in boxes and drawers. And that speaks volumes about how the child felt when he or she received it.

You are launching your students into their future.

> Bob:
> I've watched you work hard this year to achieve your goals. I know it hasn't been easy, but you have succeeded admirably. I am proud of you, and I am proud to have been your teacher.
>
> Sincerely,
>
> *Mr. Gonzales*

Dear Jessica,

Thank you for all the things you did this year that made life in room 9 so pleasant. I love the big picture and the poem you gave me. It will always remind me of the fun we had planning our model community. You were such a responsible mayor!

You are a talented and creative artist, Jessica, and a hard-working student. It has been my pleasure to have been your teacher.

Your friend,

Miss Walker

"My seven-year old daughter came running into the house waving a letter addressed to her. She kept shouting, "It's from Mrs. Montoya! It's from Mrs. Montoya!" And that's just what it was—a letter from her teacher four weeks after school was out. You should have seen the smile on her face. She must have read and re-read that letter a dozen times. Now it's pinned up on her bulletin board." —Parent

◥ Send thank-you notes to parents.

You've enlisted their support all year long. Now let them know how valuable their involvement and interest have been. This final contact from you is exceedingly important. Remember, this parent will be a parent in someone else's class next year. Do everything you can to pass along a parent who feels that his or her involvement was appreciated, and who is eager to continue that involvement.

Dear Mrs. Marcum:

This year has been especially successful for Jeff. I hope you realize what a big part you've played in that success. Once Jeff began doing his homework assignments he found he could keep up with class discussions and do better on tests. You've seen the results on his report card. Thanks again for giving him the message that homework must be done! Hope your summer is terrific.

Sincerely,

Mr Amaral

Dear Mr. and Mrs. Avery:

It's hard to believe this terrific year has ended. I have so enjoyed working with both of you. You've been generous with your time and expertise. Our World Bazaar wouldn't have been the same without the wonderful posters you painted for us. Have a wonderful summer. I look forward to seeing you at school events next year.

Sincerely,

Mrs. Pollard

Sample end-of-the-year notes to parents

Call parents with whom you've worked to solve specific problems.

Take a moment at the end of the year to think about those parents with whom you've worked to solve specific problems. These parents deserve an extra-special pat on the back for the efforts they have made on behalf of their children. Make sure they get recognition from you! Review the progress made throughout the year. If appropriate, give guidelines for continued success. Above all, thank these parents for working with you to solve their children's problems. Point out the difference their supportive involvement made.

◪ Take pride in a job well done.

You have set a new standard in education. Through your conscientious efforts to form a partnership with parents, you have demonstrated that quality education is a shared responsibility. You have taken the lead with confidence and professionalism. Be proud of your accomplishments. Know that the parents and students you have worked with will move ahead with a more positive attitude toward education. You have made a difference in the lives of your students and their parents.

You are an effective teacher.

Appendix

Power Reading Tip Sheet for Parents

See pages 78-79 for suggestions for use.

Homework Tips for Parents

See pages 101-102 for suggestions for use.

Grades 1-3

Grades 4-6

Grades 7-12

(continued)

Study Skills Tips for Parents

See pages 103-105 for suggestions for use.

How to Solve the Most Common Homework Problems

See pages 111-112 for suggestions for use.

What parents can do when:

Behavior Management Tips for Parents

See pages 179-187 for suggestions for use.

How to Power Read

Strong reading comprehension skills are the basis for success in all subject areas. You can help your child develop these skills with Power Reading. Power Reading is a technique that will help your child become a better reader by increasing both reading comprehension and listening comprehension skills. A Power Reading session takes only about fifteen minutes.

Here's how to do it:

1. Read to your child.
Read aloud to your child for five minutes. (Be sure that the book from which you are reading is at your child's reading level. If you are unsure about choosing a book, ask your child's teacher for help.) Pronounce words carefully and clearly, and make appropriate pauses for periods and commas

2. Listen to your child read.
Have your child continue reading the same book aloud. (He or she should begin at the point where you stopped reading.) Remind your child to take it slowly and read so that the words make sense.

Caution: Do not stop and correct your child while he or she is reading. If your child stumbles on a word, make a note of it and go back later.

(continued)

3. Ask questions about the material that was read.

Check how well your child was listening and reading by asking general questions about the material you read aloud and the material your child read aloud. Talk about what was read; share ideas.

Hold a Power Reading session with your child as often as possible.

It's an excellent way to improve reading skills and an excellent way to show your child the importance you place on reading. Many families have found Power Reading to be an enjoyable way to read together on a regular basis. Start a book that's of particular interest to your child and continue using this same book for Power Reading sessions until it is completed. Your child will be even more motivated to join you in Power Reading when he or she is eager to find out what happens next.

Set Up
a Study Area

To do homework successfully, your child must have a place in which to work. The study area must be well-lit, quiet, and have all necessary supplies.

Help your child choose a location at home in which homework will be done. Even if your child does most homework at another location after school, there still should be a place in the home in which he or she can study.

Remember that your child does not need a lot of space to do homework. Either the kitchen table or a corner of the living room is fine, as long as it is quiet during homework time. Whenever possible, keep the study area off limits to brothers and sisters during homework time.

PRAISE

*your child when he or she
does homework in the study area.*

Tip #2

Create a Homework Survival Kit

One of the keys to getting homework done is having supplies in one place. A Homework Survival Kit—containing supplies needed to do homework—will prevent your child from being distracted by the need to go searching for supplies, and will free you from last-minute trips to the store for folders, paper, tape and other needed items.

- If your child does homework at a location other than home (such as the library or an after-school care program) make sure that his or her homework supplies are available there.

- Respect your child's Homework Survival Kit. Don't use these supplies for other family needs.

- Give Homework Survival Kit materials as gifts. A dictionary, for example, is a special present that a child will use over and over again.

(continued)

These are the supplies needed for a Homework Survival Kit:

* pencils   * writing paper   * crayons
* markers   • ruler   • sharpener
* erasers   • glue or paste   • tape
* scissors   • stapler   • paper clips
* children's dictionary
* construction paper

*These are the most important supplies your child needs. Try to obtain these items as soon as possible. Add additional homework supplies as you are able to.

You don't need to gather all the materials in one day, but don't wait too long. Your child needs these supplies to do his or her best job on homework.

AGREE

with your child that it is his or her responsibility to remind you when any of the Homework Survival Kit materials are getting low and need replacing.

Schedule Daily Homework Time

Help your child develop good homework habits by encouraging him or her to start homework at the same time each day. By scheduling a special time for homework, you will not only help your child get work done on time, but you will also ensure that homework is done at a time when you are available to assist your child.

- It is your responsibility to schedule homework time for your child. For young children, the best time is often as soon as they (and you) arrive home at the end of the day.

- Remind your child each day when he or she is to do homework.

- Select a time when you or another responsible adult will be available to assist your child.

- Try to schedule the same homework time for all of your children. (This will make it more convenient for you to be available.)

Encourage your child to do homework
during the special homework time by giving lots of

PRAISE

each time homework is done

appropriately.

Encourage your child to work independently.

Homework teaches children responsibility. Through homework, children learn skills they must develop if they are to grow to be independent, motivated, and successful adults: how to follow directions, how to begin and complete a task, and how to manage time. By encouraging your child to work on his or her own, you are helping develop these important life skills.

Follow these guidelines:

- Check to see that your child is doing homework at the proper time.

- Suggest that your child call a friend if help is needed.

- Give your child help only if a real effort has been made to do the work.

PRAISE

your child when he or she does homework
independently. Let your child know
how proud you are!

Motivate Your Child with Praise

Children need encouragement and support from the people whose opinions they value the most—their parents. Your consistent praise can increase your child's self-confidence and motivate him or her to do the best work possible.

Try these ideas:

- Each night praise your child about some specific accomplishment, for example, "I really like how you have been doing your homework as soon as we get home."

- Use **Super Praise** to motivate your child.
  First, one parent praises the child: "I really appreciate how hard you're working to do your homework. You finished it all and you did such a nice job. Your printing is so neat and easy to read. I want to make sure Dad hears about this."

  Second, this parent praises the child in front of the other parent: "Amanda did a wonderful job on her homework today. She started it without complaining, she stayed with it, and she did a super job on it."

  Finally, the other person praises the child: "I feel so proud of you, getting such a good report from Mom. You're really doing fine!"

If you're a single parent, you can use a grandparent, a neighbor, or a family friend as your partner in delivering Super Praise. Any adult whose approval your child will value can fill the role of the second person offering praise.

Set Up a Study Area

To do homework successfully, your child must have a place in which to work. The study area must be well-lit, quiet, and have all necessary supplies.

Help your child choose a location at home in which homework will be done. Even if your child does most homework at another location after school, there still should be a place in the home in which he or she can study.

Remember that your child does not need a lot of space to do homework. Either the kitchen table or a corner of the living room is fine, as long as it is quiet during homework time. Whenever possible, keep the study area off limits to brothers and sisters during homework time.

PRAISE

*your child when he or she
does homework in the study area.*

Create a Homework Survival Kit

One of the keys to getting homework done is having supplies in one place. A Homework Survival Kit—containing supplies needed to do homework—will prevent your child from being distracted by the need to go searching for supplies, and will free you from last-minute trips to the store for folders, paper, tape and other needed items.

- If your child does homework at a location other than home (such as the library or an after-school care program) make sure that his or her homework supplies are available there.

- Respect your child's Homework Survival Kit. Don't use these supplies for other family needs.

- Give Homework Survival Kit materials as gifts. A dictionary, for example, is a special present that a child will use over and over again.

(continued)

These are the supplies needed for a Homework Survival Kit:

* pencils
* writing paper
• crayons
• ruler
• pencil sharpener
• tape
• scissors
• paper clips
• index cards
• glue or paste

* pens
• colored pencils
• markers
• erasers
• hole punch
• stapler
• folders for reports
• assignment book
• dictionary
• construction paper

*These are the most important supplies your child needs. Try to obtain these items as soon as possible. Add additional homework supplies as you are able to.

You don't need to gather all the materials in one day, but don't wait too long. Your child needs these supplies to do his or her best job on homework.

AGREE

with your child that it is his or her responsibility to remind you when any of the Homework Survival Kit materials are getting low and need replacing.

Tip #3

Schedule Daily Homework Time

Help your child develop good homework habits by encouraging him or her to start homework at the same time each day. By scheduling Daily Homework Time, you will not only help your child get work done on time, but you can also ensure that homework is done at a time when you are available to assist your child.

Daily Homework Time is a time set aside each day during which your child must do homework. During Daily Homework Time all other activities must stop; your child must go to his or her study area and get to work.

Here's how to introduce Daily Homework Time:

1 Tell your child that homework is to be done at the same time each day, during Daily Homework Time.

2 Help your child determine the length of time needed each day for homework.

3 Have your child write down his scheduled after-school activities and responsibilities in the designated spaces on the Daily Schedule.

(continued)

4 Encourage your child to identify his or her best time for doing homework. (Example: right after school vs right after dinner) Then tell your child to determine the best time period each day to be set aside for Daily Homework Time.

5 Have your child write the Daily Homework Time in the spaces shown on the Daily Schedule.

6 Check your child's completed Daily Schedule for accuracy. Make sure that the homework times chosen are appropriate.

7 Post the Daily Schedule in a prominent location. Encourage your child to stick to the schedule!

PRAISE

your child when homework is completed during Daily Homework Time.

(continued)

Daily Schedule

Monday Homework Time:

3:00 PM	7:00 PM
4:00 PM	8:00 PM
5:00 PM	9:00 PM
6:00 PM	10:00 PM

Tuesday Homework Time:

3:00 PM	7:00 PM
4:00 PM	8:00 PM
5:00 PM	9:00 PM
6:00 PM	10:00 PM

Wednesday Homework Time:

3:00 PM	7:00 PM
4:00 PM	8:00 PM
5:00 PM	9:00 PM
6:00 PM	10:00 PM

Thursday Homework Time:

3:00 PM	7:00 PM
4:00 PM	8:00 PM
5:00 PM	9:00 PM
6:00 PM	10:00 PM

Friday Homework Time:

3:00 PM	7:00 PM
4:00 PM	8:00 PM
5:00 PM	9:00 PM
6:00 PM	10:00 PM

Encourage your child to work independently.

Homework teaches children responsibility. Through homework, children learn skills they must develop if they are to grow to be independent, motivated, and successful adults: how to follow directions, how to begin and complete a task, and how to manage time. By encouraging your child to work on his or her own, you are helping develop these important life skills.

Follow these guidelines:

- Check to see that your child is doing homework at the proper time.

- Suggest that your child call a friend if help is needed.

- Give your child help only if a real effort has been made to do the work.

PRAISE

*your child when he or she does
homework independently. Let your child
know how proud you are!*

Grades 4-6

**Homework
Tips**
for Parents

Tip #5

Motivate Your Child with Praise

Children need encouragement and support from the people whose opinions they value the most—their parents. Your consistent praise can increase your child's self-confidence and motivate him or her to do the best work possible.

Try these ideas:

• Each night praise your child about some specific accomplishment, for example, "I really like how you have been completing your homework each night."

• Use **Super Praise** to motivate your child.

   First, one parent praises the child: "I really appreciate how hard you're working to do your homework. You finished it all and you did such a great job. I want to make sure Dad hears about this."

   Second, this parent praises the child in front of the other parent: "Amanda did a really wonderful job on her homework today. She started it without complaining, she stayed with it, and she did a super job on it."

   Finally, the other person praises the child: "I really feel proud of you, getting such a good report from Mom. You're really doing fine!"

If you're a single parent, you can use a grandparent, a neighbor, or a family friend as your partner in delivering Super Praise. Any adult whose approval your child will value can fill the role of the second person offering praise.

Parents On Your Side © Lee Canter & Associates

Set Up a Study Area

To do homework successfully, your child must have a place in which to work. The study area must be well-lit, quiet, and have all necessary supplies.

Have your child choose a location at home in which homework will be done. Even if your child does most homework at another location after school, there still should be a place in the home in which he or she can study.

Remember that your child does not need a lot of space to do homework. The kitchen table or a corner of the living room is fine, as long as it is quiet during homework time. Whenever possible, keep the study area off limits to brothers and sisters during homework time

PRAISE

*your child when he or she
does homework in the study area.*

Create a Homework Survival Kit

One of the keys to getting homework done is having supplies in one place. A Homework Survival Kit—containing supplies needed to do homework—will prevent your child from being distracted by the need to go searching for supplies, and will free you or your child from last-minute trips to the store for folders, paper, tape and other needed items.

These are the supplies needed for a Homework Survival Kit:

* pencils
* writing paper
• colored pencils
• markers
• sharpener
• glue
• stapler
• paper clips
• almanac
• protractor

* pens
* assignment book
• white out
• ruler
• erasers
• tape
• scissors
• dictionary
• thesaurus
• compass

(continued)

- Your child doesn't need to run out and get all of the supplies immediately. A completed Homework Survival Kit is a goal to work toward. Start by gathering the items marked by an asterisk (*). Get other supplies as you are able.

- Respect your child's Homework Survival Kit. Don't use these supplies for other family needs.

- Give Homework Survival Kit materials as gifts. A dictionary, for example, is a special present that a child will use over and over again.

AGREE

with your child that it is his or her responsibility to keep track of the Homework Survival Kit materials that are getting low and need replacing.

**Homework
Tips**
for Parents

Tip #3

Schedule Daily Homework Time

Help your child develop good homework habits by encouraging him or her to start homework at the same time each day. Daily Homework Time is a time set aside each day during which your child must do homework. During Daily Homework Time all other activities must stop; your child must go to his or her study area and get to work.

Here's how to introduce Daily Homework Time:

1 Tell your child that homework is to be done at the same time each day, during Daily Homework Time.

2 Help your child determine the length of time needed each day for homework.

3 Have your child write down his scheduled after-school activities and responsibilities in the designated spaces on the Daily Schedule.

(continued)

4 Encourage your child to identify his or her best time for doing homework. (Example: right after school vs right after dinner) Then tell your child to determine the best time period each day to be set aside for Daily Homework Time.

5 Have your child write the Daily Homework Time in the spaces shown on the Daily Schedule.

6 Check your child's completed Daily Schedule for accuracy. Make sure that the homework times chosen are appropriate.

7 Post the Daily Schedule in a prominent location. Encourage your child to stick to the schedule!

PRAISE

your child when homework is completed during
Daily Homework Time.

(continued)

Daily Schedule

Monday Homework Time:

3:00 PM	7:00 PM
4:00 PM	8:00 PM
5:00 PM	9:00 PM
6:00 PM	10:00 PM

Tuesday Homework Time:

3:00 PM	7:00 PM
4:00 PM	8:00 PM
5:00 PM	9:00 PM
6:00 PM	10:00 PM

Wednesday Homework Time:

3:00 PM	7:00 PM
4:00 PM	8:00 PM
5:00 PM	9:00 PM
6:00 PM	10:00 PM

Thursday Homework Time:

3:00 PM	7:00 PM
4:00 PM	8:00 PM
5:00 PM	9:00 PM
6:00 PM	10:00 PM

Friday Homework Time:

3:00 PM	7:00 PM
4:00 PM	8:00 PM
5:00 PM	9:00 PM
6:00 PM	10:00 PM

Encourage your child to work independently.

Homework teaches children responsibility. Through homework, children learn skills they must develop if they are to grow to be independent, motivated, and successful adults, capable of handling a job: how to follow directions, how to begin and complete a task, and how to manage time. By encouraging your child to work on his or her own, you are helping develop these important life skills.

Follow these guidelines:

- Check to see that your child is doing homework at the proper time.

- Suggest that your child call a friend if help is needed.

- Give your child help only if a real effort has been made to do the work.

PRAISE

your child when he or she does homework independently. Let your child know how proud you are!

Motivate Your Child with Praise

Children need encouragement and support from the people whose opinions they value the most—their parents. Your consistent praise can increase your child's self-confidence and motivate him or her to do the best work possible.

Try these ideas:

- Each night praise your child about some specific accomplishment. Example: "I really am proud of the way you have met your research paper deadlines. This rough draft is excellent!"

- Use **Super Praise** to motivate your child.
  First, one parent praises the child: "I've noticed how hard you're working to do your homework each night. You're doing your work on your own and getting assignments done on time. I'll make sure Mom hears about this when she gets home."
  Second, this parent praises the child in front of the other parent: "I thought you'd like to know that Bob is doing a great job on homework. He's taking responsibility for his work, and completing it on time."

  Finally, the other person praises the child: "I'm so proud of you, getting such a good report from Dad. You're really doing great!"

If you're a single parent, you can use a grandparent, a neighbor, or a family friend as your partner in delivering Super Praise. Any adult whose approval your child will value can fill the role of the second person offering praise.

How to Help with Long-Range Planning

A Long-Range Planner can teach your child how to successfully complete longer projects. By using the Long-Range Planner, your child will learn how to break down a big project into small, easily completed tasks.

Using the Long-Range Planner

When your child brings home a long-range project, take time to help him or her determine the steps that have to be

1 Break down your BIG assignments into all of the smaller steps it takes to get the project done.
2 Write down your "mini" due dates for each step.
3 Fill in the final due date for the project on your last step.

LONG-RANGE PLANNER

Assignment Term report   Due Date 3/6

1 Pick out the topic of the report.   Due Date 2/2

2 Do fact-finding research   Due Date 2/11

3 Decide what questions I want to answer in report.   Due Date 2/15

4 Take notes about the topic.   Due Date 2/22

5 Write the rough draft.   Due Date 2/29

6 Write the final draft.   Due Date 3/6

7   Due Date

followed to complete the project. Once the assignment has been broken down into more easily managed steps, work together to establish the time period in which each step will be completed. Write the steps and the dates of completion on the Long-Range Planner. If each goal is met, there will be no last-minute panic before the report is due. See the example on this page of a completed Long-Range Planner for a term report.

(continued)

1 Break down your BIG assignments into all of the smaller steps it takes to get the project done.

2 Write down your "mini" due dates for each step.

3 Fill in the final due date for the project on your last step.

LONG-RANGE PLANNER

Assignment _____ **Due Date** _____

_____

1 _____ Due Date _____

_____

2 _____ Due Date _____

_____

3 _____ Due Date _____

_____

4 _____ Due Date _____

_____

5 _____ Due Date _____

_____

6 _____ Due Date _____

_____

7 _____ Due Date _____

_____

How to Help with Written Reports

Reports are often difficult for students to handle in an organized manner. Here are some suggestions that will help you encourage your child to perform at top capacity.

Use the Long-Range Planner

Planning is an important part of getting a written report done on time. If a term paper is left until the last minute, it is very unlikely that best-effort work will result. Using a Long-Range Planner can ensure that the project will be well thought out and completed on time.

Use a Written Report Checklist

Before your child writes a report, encourage him or her to fill out a Written Report Checklist. By answering the questions on the checklist before beginning to write, your child will prevent many unnecessary errors and rewrites.

Use a Proofreading Checklist

Proofreading is an important step in completing any written assignment. You can help your child develop better proofreading skills by providing the Proofreading Checklist included here. Make copies of the checklist so that there will always be plenty available at home. Make sure that your child understands that each draft of a written assignment should be proofread.

(continued)

Whenever a report is assigned, take time to check off or write down the requirements. Make copies of this checklist and keep them available for use.

WRITTEN REPORT CHECKLIST

Subject of Report _____

Date Report Is Due_____

1 How long should the report be?
How many paragraphs____or pages____do I need to write?

2 Should the report be typewritten or handwritten?
Typewritten ☐   Pen ☐   Pencil☐

3 Should I write or type on every line or every other line?
Every line ☐   Every other line ☐

4 Should I write or type on one side of the page or on both?
One side ☐   Both sides ☐

5 Where should I put the page numbers on each page?
Top ☐   Left ☐   Center ☐   Right ☐
Bottom ☐   Left ☐   Center ☐   Right ☐

6 Should I put the report in a folder?
Yes ☐   No ☐

7 Should I add photos or illustrations?
Photos ☐   Illustrations ☐
Other _____

Additional notes: _____
_____
_____

Use the Proofreading Checklist each time you complete a rough draft and again after your final draft.

PROOFREADING CHECKLIST

Subject of Report _____
Date Report Is Due _____

_____ The title of the paper is suited to the subject.

_____ The paper is well organized with a clear introduction.

_____ I have put in all capital letters, commas, periods and apostrophes where needed.

_____ Every sentence is a complete sentence.

_____ Each paragraph has a topic sentence that tells what the paragraph will be about.

_____ I have used descriptive words to make my paper more interesting.

_____ The paper contains specific facts and information about the subject.

_____ I have read my paper aloud, or reread it, and it says what I want it to say.

_____ The last sentence of the paper lets the reader know that the paper is finished.

_____ I have done at least one rough draft of the paper.

_____ I have checked the final paper for spelling errors.

_____ This is my best work.

How to Help Your Child Study for Tests

Part One: What To Do First

Step 1: Determine what the test will cover and organize all study materials.

Your child needs to know exactly what material a test will cover: chapters in the textbook, class notes, homework assignments, etc. Your child will study more successfully if he or she has organized all the materials that will be covered on the test and has them available for study.

Step 2: Schedule time for studying.

Your child needs to plan study time carefully to make sure enough time has been allowed to prepare for the test. Break down study tasks throughout the week. It is better to study a little bit each day than to cram on the night before a test.

Step 3: Use effective study techniques.

The following study techniques can help your child study more successfully.

Write important information on index cards.

A supply of 3" x 5" index cards should always be available at home. As your child studies, he or she should summarize important information and write

(continued)

it on index cards. Later, these cards can be used to review for the test.

Review homework and class notes.

All homework and class notes should be reviewed before a test. It is helpful to underline or highlight important points.

Review study questions, past quizzes and tests.

It's always a good idea to look over past tests and quizzes. They might give clues about what to expect on future tests. Did the teacher ask multiple-choice questions? True/False questions? Essay questions? Make sure your child also spends time reviewing the study questions in the textbook. These questions provide an excellent review of the material covered.

Make a list of sample test questions.

Have your child make up a list of test questions that might show up on the test. Then have him or her prepare answers for these questions. Chances are, a lot of the questions will be given on the test.

Part 2: How to Study a Textbook

Often most of the material covered on a test will be from assigned reading in the class textbook. Here is a step-by-step plan that will enable your child to master the material in any textbook.

Step 1: Survey the chapter.
The first step in studying a textbook is to survey the chapter. Have your child follow these steps:

1 Read all headings and subheadings.
2 Look over all pictures, maps, charts, tables and graphs.
3 Read the summary at the end of the chapter.

(continued)

4 Read through the study questions listed at the end of the chapter.
5 Finally, go back and make up a question from each main heading.

Step 2: Read the chapter and take notes.

After your child has surveyed the chapter, he or she should go back and read it all the way through. Notes should be taken on a separate sheet of paper. These notes should include:

- Answers to the questions, made from the chapter headings.
- A chronological listing of events that occur in the chapter.

In addition, your child should take notes on index cards. Important facts (names of persons, terms to know, or significant concepts) are listed on the front of the card. The back should be used for listing important points that may be asked on the test.

Step 3: Review the chapter.

After your child finishes reading the chapter, he or she should look over the notes and make sure all the main points are understood. Then your child should answer the study questions given at the end of the chapter, as well as the questions formulated from the main headings. He or she should review all the notes and all the key points of the chapter.

(continued)

Use this checklist to help you make sure you've covered all the important points of a chapter. Check off each item after you've completed it.

TEXTBOOK STUDY CHECKLIST

Textbook _____

Chapter _____

SURVEY THE CHAPTER

____ Read all major headings and subheadings.

____ Note all pictures, maps, charts, tables, graphs, etc.

____ Read the summary at the end of the chapter.

____ Read the study questions listed at the end of the chapter.

MAKE QUESTIONS OF MAJOR HEADINGS

____ Go through the chapter and reword all main headings into study questions to be answered.

READ THE CHAPTER AND TAKE NOTES

____ Answer all the questions you made of the main headings.

____ Take notes on a separate piece of paper.

____ List important events, concepts or facts in order.

____ Make 3" x 5" index cards of important terms, people and events.

REVIEW THE CHAPTER

____ Make sure you understand all the main points and how they related to one another.

____ Answer all the study questions at the end of the chapter.

____ Review notes to make sure all key points have been covered.

For the parent(s) of_____

Homework is an excellent way to teach your child the importance of starting, staying with and completing a job. It is also an opportunity to teach your child to do the best work he or she can. But your child may rush through homework in order to talk on the phone, watch TV, or get together with friends. You need to let your child know that doing homework and doing it well is a responsibility. Letting your child rush through an assignment or do sloppy work is teaching that it is all right not to do his or her best work.

Here's what to do when your child doesn't do his or her best work:

1   Schedule Daily Homework Time.
Daily Homework Time is a time set aside each day during which your child must do homework. During Daily Homework Time, all other activities must stop; your child must go to his or her study area and get to work. Tell your child that homework is to be done during a regularly scheduled Daily Homework Time.

2   Tell your child what you expect.
"I have been looking at your homework assignments and I know you can do a better job. You are not to rush through your assignments. I want you to take your time and do the best work you can. Sloppy work with a lot of mistakes is not acceptable."

3   Praise your child for work done well.
Simply telling your child what you expect may be enough to inspire better work. If so, make sure that you recognize it! After you have talked with your child, check the next assignment. If the work is better, praise your child by saying things like, "Great job getting your homework done," or "I like how neat your work is today. Keep up the good work." Praising your child for good work is the best way to encourage continued best efforts.

(continued)

4   Institute Mandatory Homework Time.
If your child still rushes through homework, it is probably because the faster it is done the more time he or she will have to spend with friends or watch TV. Mandatory Homework Time takes away these advantages of getting homework done as fast as possible.

Mandatory Homework Time means that a child must use the entire scheduled Daily Homework Time for homework or other academic activities whether or not homework is completed. In other words, if two hours is allotted each night, the entire two hours must be spent on homework. If homework is finished, the rest of the time must be spent on other academic work such as reading, reviewing textbooks or practicing math. When children learn that rushing through homework will not be rewarded with more free time, they will learn quickly to slow down and do a better job.

5   Provide additional incentives.
To encourage your child to continue good work, give a reward or a point toward a prize each time homework is completed. For instance, each night he or she does a good job on homework, one point is earned. When five points are earned reward your child with an extra privilege.

6   Contact the teacher.
If after trying these five steps your child is still not doing his or her best work, contact the teacher. You and the teacher must work together to improve your child's performance.

It is important that you encourage your child to take care and do a good job on homework. If your child learns that it is all right not to do his or her best work, that attitude can be carried outside of school to a job where a boss is much less sympathetic about sloppy work.

For the parent(s) of_____

When your child would rather battle with you every night than do homework, it is time to set firm limits. Your child may openly refuse to do homework or lie to you or to the teacher about why it hasn't been done. To solve this problem, you must make it clear to your child that choosing not to do homework is choosing not to enjoy certain privileges.

Here's what to do when your child refuses to do homework assignments:

1   State clearly how you expect homework to be completed.
Tell your child, "I expect you to do all of your homework every night. Under no circumstances will I tolerate your refusing to do your homework assignments."

2   Back up your words with actions.
When your child is in a power struggle with you and refuses to do homework, you must make it clear that his or her behavior will result in a loss of privileges. Tell your child, "You can choose either to do your homework or to not have privileges. If you choose not to do your homework, then, until you have finished your assignments, you will lose these privileges: You will not leave this house. You will not watch TV. You will not be allowed to listen to music or use the telephone. You will sit here until all of your homework is done. The choice is yours." Then, stick with your demands. It may take your child several days of sitting idly in his or her study area to realize that you mean business.

3   Praise your child when homework is done.
Praise your child each time he or she completes homework. "I really like the way you've been getting your homework done. That's what I expect from you."

(continued)

4   Use a Homework Contract.
A Homework Contract is an effective motivator for young people of any age. A Homework Contract is an agreement between you and your child that states: "When you do your homework, you will earn a reward." For example: "Each day that you bring home your homework and complete it appropriately, you will earn one point. When you have earned five points (or ten points) you will earn a special privilege." (The younger the child, the more quickly he or she should be able to earn the reward.)

5   Contact the teacher.
If problems continue, contact the teacher and request that additional discipline be provided at school for homework assignments not completed. Your child will quickly learn that the school is backing up your efforts.

Your child must learn that homework is not a battleground. There can be no power struggle over homework. It must be done. Your child must learn that conflict on this issue will not be tolerated.

For the parent(s) of_____

From time to time your child may forget to bring home books or homework assignments. But when he or she continually fails to bring home assigned homework, you must take action.

Here's what to do when your child fails to bring assignments home:

1 State clearly that you expect all homework assignments to be brought home.

Tell your child, "I expect you to bring home all your assigned work and all the books you need to complete your assignments. If you finish your homework during free time at school, I expect you to bring it home so that I can see it."

2 Work with the teacher(s) to make sure you know what homework has been assigned.

Students should be writing all homework assignments down on a weekly assignment sheet. Ask your child's teacher(s) to check and sign the assignment sheet at the end of class. When your child completes the assignments, you sign the sheet and have your child return it to the teacher.

3 Provide praise and support when all homework assignments are brought home.

Make sure that your child knows that you appreciate it every time he or she brings home all homework assignments. "It's great to see that you remembered to bring home all of your homework. I knew you could do it."

4 Institute Mandatory Homework Time.

If your child still fails to bring home assignments, he or she may be avoiding homework in favor of spending time with friends or watching TV. Mandatory Homework Time eliminates the advantages of forgetting homework.

(continued)

Mandatory Homework Time means that your child must spend a specific amount of time on academic activities whether homework is brought home or not. In other words, if one hour (or two) is allotted each night for homework, the entire time must be spent on academic work such as reading, or reviewing textbooks or class notes. When students learn that their irresponsible approach to homework will not be rewarded with more free time, they will quickly learn to remember to bring home their assignments.

5   Use a Homework Contract.
A Homework Contract is an effective motivator for young people of any age. A Homework Contract is an agreement between you and your child that states: "When you do your homework, you will earn a reward." For example: "Each day that you bring home your homework and complete it appropriately, you will earn one point. When you have earned five points (or ten points) you will earn a special privilege." (The younger the child, the more quickly he or she should be able to earn the reward.)

6   Work with the teacher to follow through at school for homework not completed.
If your child continues to forget homework, discuss with the teacher the possibility of imposing loss of privileges at school. Loss of lunch time, or assigning after-school detention lets your child know that you and the school are working together to ensure that he or she behaves responsibly.

Your child must learn to bring home and complete all homework assignments. Accept no excuses.

For the parent(s) of_____

Some children spend hours and hours on homework when it is really not necessary. They may stop and start and be easily distracted. When your child takes the entire evening to do homework, you need to step in and help solve the problem.

Here's what to do when your child takes all night to do homework:

1   Schedule Daily Homework Time.
Daily Homework Time is a time set aside each day during which your child must do homework. During Daily Homework Time all other activities must stop; your child must go to his or her study area and get to work. Tell your child that homework is to be done during a regularly scheduled Daily Homework Time. Say to your child, "I expect you to get all of your homework done during Daily Homework Time. Your taking all evening to do it must stop at once.

2   Make sure that homework is being done in a quiet study area.
Your child may take too much time to do homework because he or she is working in a distracting environment. Make sure that during homework time your child has no access to TV, stereo, or other distractions and is not disturbed by brothers and sisters. You may wish to change the location of the study area if such distractions are present.

3   Give praise and support when your child does homework on time.
Let your child feel your approval each time homework is finished during homework time. "Great job! I am really pleased to see that you got your homework done on time. I'm so proud of you!"

(continued)

4   Give additional incentives when appropriate.
Your child may need extra help to develop the habit of getting homework done promptly. A good incentive for solving this particular problem is the Beat the Clock game. To play this game with your child, you first determine how long it should take for the child to finish the homework. Then at the start of homework time, a timer is set. If the child finishes the homework appropriately within the given time, a special privilege is earned.

5   Back up your words with actions.
If the first four steps do not succeed in getting your child to finish homework during homework time, you must take a stand. Tell your child: "You have a choice. You can do your homework during homework time or you can choose not have certain privileges. If you choose not to do your homework, then from the beginning of homework time until you have finished your homework, you will lose these privileges: You will not leave this house. You will not watch TV. You will not be allowed to listen to music. You will not be allowed to use the telephone to either make or receive calls. You will sit there until your homework is finished. The choice is yours."

Learning to do homework responsibly is an important part of growing into responsible adulthood.

If your child will not do homework without your assistance, you must make sure that he or she is making a genuine effort in trying to work alone. If your child insists that you sit with him or her all night or continually begs for your assistance, follow the steps below:

Here's what to do when your child will not do homework on his or her own:

1   State clearly that you expect your child to work alone.
Tell your child: "I expect you to do your homework without my help. I will not sit with you or do your work for you. I will not be available to answer questions every five minutes."

2   Schedule Daily Homework Time.
Daily Homework Time is a time set aside each day during which your child must do homework. During Daily Homework Time all other activities must stop; your child must go to his or her study area and get to work. Tell your child that homework is to be done during a regularly scheduled Daily Homework Time.

3   Give praise and support when your child works on his or her own.
Monitor your child during homework time. When you see your child working alone, say: "I am really proud of the way you are doing all of this work on your own. I knew you could do it!"

4   Help your child build confidence.
Many children will not work without your help because they feel their homework assignments are just too much to handle on their own. "Chunking" is a great way to help your child gain the confidence needed to work on his or her own. "Chunking" means dividing a big

(continued)

assignment into smaller chunks you know can be handled successfully. For example, a 20-problem math assignment would be broken into five chunks of four problems each. The child is rewarded with a prize (raisins, peanuts, etc.) each time one of the chunks is completed until the assignment is finished.

5   **Help your child only after he or she has genuinely tried to solve the problem on his or her own.**
Be sure that your child has tried the problem at least twice before you agree to help. There will be times when something is really too hard for your child to understand, but be sure that you don't step in until he or she has made a genuine effort to solve the problem.

6   **Give additional incentives when appropriate.**
Another technique to help children work on their own is "Trade-Off." With this game, place a bowl of small candies, raisins or peanuts in front of your child and say: "Each time you ask me for help with your homework, you will have to give me one of these candies (raisins, etc.). When they are all gone, I won't help you anymore. At the end of homework time, you get to keep what's left."

7   **Back up your words with action.**
If the first six steps do not succeed in getting your child to work without your help, it's time to be firm. Make sure that your child knows that at the end of homework time you will no longer be available to help and that your child will sit in his or her work space until the work is done—even if it means remaining there all evening. Be prepared for your child to use anger, tears or indifference to manipulate you into backing down. Let your child know that such tactics will not work and he or she will remain in the study area until he or she learns to work alone.

Children must learn to do homework on their own. Relying on you for help will only lead to greater dependence. Your child must develop the confidence to tackle any homework assignment.

For the parent(s) of_____

If your child puts off starting long-range assignments until just before they are due, it can put stress on the entire family. Typically, this child waits until the last minute and then goes into a frenzy, demanding your immediate help. To solve this problem, you must take steps to teach your child about long-range planning.

Here's what to do when your child waits until the last minute to finish assignments:

1   State clearly that you expect long-range projects to be planned and completed responsibly.
Sit down with your child and say that you will not tolerate putting off projects until just before they are due: "I expect you to plan your book reports (term papers, etc.) responsibly. This waiting until the last minute must stop."

2   Ask the teacher for a Long-Range Planner.
Ask your child's teacher to give your child a Long-Range Planner. By using the Long-Range Planner, your child will learn how to break down a large project into small, easily completed tasks and how to distribute the assignment over the period of time given for the project. Insist that your child tell you about each long-range assignment and then help your child use the planner to decide when each step of the project is to be completed.

3   Give praise and support for your child as each step is completed.
Each time your child completes a step of a long-range project, express your approval: "I think that it is wonderful that you picked out the book for your report so quickly." "I really like how you finished reading the book before the date you scheduled! Keep up the good work."

(continued)

4   Give additional motivators when appropriate.
If your child needs additional motivation to complete a long-range project on time, institute a system·that allows your child to earn a point toward a reward or privilege each time a step is completed according to the schedule.

5   Back up your words with action.
If the first four steps fail to motivate your child to do long-range planning, it's time to impose restrictions. If your child fails to read a book selected for a book report by the agreed-upon date, take away a privilege (watching TV, using the phone) until the book is read. Unless you set limits, your child is not going to believe that you mean business.

Your child must learn to budget the time allocated for long-range projects. It's a skill that must be developed if your child is to be capable of taking on larger tasks as he or she grows up.

For the parent(s) of_____

Solving Homework Problems

If your child will not do homework unless there is a parent at home, you must take steps to help your child develop a more responsible approach to homework.

Here's what to do when your child will not do homework if you're not home:

1   State clearly that you expect homework to be done whether you are home or not.
Tell your child: "I expect you to get your homework done every night whether or not I am home."

2   Schedule Daily Homework Time.
Daily Homework Time is a time set aside each day during which your child must do homework. During Daily Homework Time all other activities must stop; your child must go to his or her study area and get to work. Tell your child that homework is to be done during a regularly scheduled Daily Homework Time.

3   If appropriate, make sure the person responsible for child care knows about Daily Homework Time.
Make sure that the person responsible for your child's care knows *where* your child is expected to do homework and *when* homework is to be done. It is a good idea to sit down with your child and the caregiver and let both know that you expect homework to be done just as though you were home.

4   Monitor your child when you're not home to make sure homework is done.
Telephone your child at the beginning of Daily Homework Time to be sure homework has begun. Call back, if possible, at the end of Daily Homework Time to make sure your child has completed the assignments. Have

(continued)

your child leave completed homework out for you to check when you get home. You may phase out this monitoring as your child begins to work responsibly.

5   Give praise and positive support.
Praise your child for homework done in your absence. When you call at the start of Daily Homework Time and find that your child has started on time, say: "I really like the way you got started so promptly, even without my being there." When you get home and find homework completed, tell your child: "Great! You are doing such a good job on your homework when I am not here. Keep up the terrific work!"

6   Use additional incentives when necessary.
Special incentives may be necessary at first to get your child into the habit of doing homework without your supervision. A Homework Contract is an effective motivator that can work well with children of any age.

A Homework Contract states:

• That homework will be done whether you are home or not.

• The amount of time in which homework is to be completed.

• The number of points earned each time the child completes homework.

• The reward the child will receive when a certain number of points is earned.

For example, a child might receive one point each night homework is completed. When five points are reached, a reward is earned.

7   Back up your words with action.
If the first six steps do not work, tell your child that he or she is required to sit in the study area until homework is

(continued)

finished, whether you are home or not. Tell the child: "You have a choice. You can do your homework during Daily Homework Time or you can choose not to have privileges. If you choose not to do your homework, then from the beginning of Daily Homework Time until you have finished your homework, you will lose these privileges: You will not leave this house. You will not watch TV. You will not listen to music. You will sit there until homework is finished. The choice is yours."

If there is no one providing child care, you may have to impose backup disciplinary consequences as soon as you get home. If you find homework not completed, turn off the TV, get your child off the phone, and make sure he or she gets back to work.

8 **Work with the teacher to take action at school for homework not completed.**
If your child continues to not complete homework, discuss with the teacher the possibility of imposing loss of privileges at school. Loss of recess or lunch time or after-school detention lets your child know that you and the school are working together to ensure that he or she behaves responsibly.

Regardless of whether or not you're home, your child must realize that he or she is responsible for finishing all homework assignments. Your child must learn that irresponsibility about homework is unacceptable.

How to Help Your Child Behave in School

Here are five common-sense techniques that will help you motivate your child to behave in school.

1. Tell your child how you expect him or her to behave in school.

Speak clearly and directly. Sit down with your child and in a no-nonsense, serious manner let him or her know that you are the parent, and you set the rules. Look your child in the eyes and say: "There is no way I am going to tolerate your misbehavior at school. I know that you can behave. And I care about you and love you too much to allow you to continue acting this way at school."

It is very important that you remain calm while speaking. Don't yell or scream your demands. Speak in a firm, clear tone of voice. By staying calm you will let your child know you are in control.

2. Avoid arguments. Use the Broken-Record technique.

When you tell your child to do something, chances are you'll get an argument back. Don't fall into the trap of arguing with your child! Arguing is not useful. Nobody wins. You must stick to your point and let your child know that you mean business. A technique called the Broken Record will help you avoid fruitless arguments.

(continued)

Here's how to use the Broken-Record technique:

First, tell your child exactly what you want him or her to do. For example,

"I expect you to complete your assignments during class."

If your child argues, just keep repeating what you want. Do not respond to anything your child says. Just say, "I understand, but I want you to complete your assignments in class."

Use the Broken Record a maximum of three times. If it does not work, stop the conversation. If the problem persists, you will have to take stronger actions. You will need to back up your words with actions.

3. Back up your words with actions.

If your child chooses to continue to misbehave, you must be ready to back up your words with actions. This means that you must have disciplinary consequences chosen that you will use if your child still does not behave. The consequence must be something that your child does not like, but it must not be physically or psychologically harmful. Taking away privileges, such as watching TV or talking on the phone is often effective. So is grounding. With younger children, grounding can mean being restricted to their room for a specific amount of time. For older children, grounding can mean having to say at home for a certain number of days.

Follow these guidelines:

• **Always present the consequence as a choice.**
Your child must understand that he or she has a choice. Your child can behave as you ask, or misbehave and choose to accept the consequence.

(continued)

Tell your child: "If you misbehave at school, you will choose to (for example) lose the privilege of watching TV during the week."

• **Give the child the consequence each time he or she chooses to misbehave.**
You must be consistent if your child is to know that you mean business. Each time your child chooses to misbehave at school he or she must be given the consequence. No exceptions. No excuses. Don't back down.

• **Stay calm when you give the consequence.**
Stay in control. Remember, your child chose this to happen. You are simply following through with what you promised.

• **Forgive and forget.**
Once your child has received the consequence, the issue is over and should be forgotten. It's time to move on. Don't stay angry or resentful. Instead, let your child know that you still have confidence in his or her ability to behave appropriately.

4. Know what to do when your child begins testing you.

Children often test their parents to see if they really mean business. Don't be surprised if this happens to you. When given a consequence, your child may cry, scream or yell at you, or beg you to give him or her just one more chance. Stand your ground! No matter how much your child cries or pleads, you must follow through with the consequence. Don't give in, no matter how upset your child gets. Let your child know that you are prepared to follow through.

Tell your child: (for example) "You have chosen to be grounded in your room. You will go to your room and stay there."

(continued)

5. Catch your child being good.

Praise your child when he or she behaves appropriately at school! This is the real key to improving behavior. All children appreciate hearing praise from parents, and yours is no exception.

Follow these guidelines:

First, give your child plenty of praise when he or she begins to show improvement. You need to let your child know that you recognize the good effort being made. Don't ever let a day of good behavior go unrecognized.

Tell your child: "I like how well you did at school today. I'm so proud of you for trying so hard."

Next, keep in mind that sometimes it's helpful to combine your praise with special privileges or rewards, like staying up late one night, going out to lunch, or going to a movie—whatever your child might appreciate and you are comfortable giving. Ask yourself, "What would my child like to earn? What special treat might make him or her put in a bit more effort?"

Be consistent in giving praise.

Your child must know that, just as he or she can expect disciplinary consequences for misbehavior, he or she can also expect lots of praise and reinforcement for good behavior.

Parents On Your Side © Lee Canter & Associates

Bibliography

Barth, R. (1979) "Home-based Reinforcement of School Behavior: A Review and Analysis," *Review of Educational Research*, vol. 49, No. 3, 436-458.

Bronfenbrenner, Urie. (1966) *A Report on Longitudinal Evaluations of Pre-School Programs*. Washington, D.C.: Department of Health, Education.

Brookover, W.B. and Gigliotti, R.J. (1988) *First Teachers: Parental Involvement in the Public Schools*. Alexandria, VA: National School Boards Association.

Bumstead, R.A. (1982) "Public Or Private? What Parents Want from Their Schools," *Principal*, March 1982, 39-43.

Canter, L. and Canter, M. (1976) *Assertive Discipline—A Take-Charge Approach for Today's Educator*. Santa Monica, CA: Lee Canter & Associates.

Canter, L. and Canter, M. (1985) *Assertive Discipline Resource Materials Workbook*. Santa Monica, CA: Lee Canter & Associates.

Canter, L. and Canter, M. (1988) *Assertive Discipline For Parents*. New York, NY: Harper & Row.

Canter, L. (1988) *Parent Conference Book*. Santa Monica, CA: Lee Canter & Associates.

Canter, L. and Hausner, L., Ph.D. (1987) *Homework Without Tears*. New York, NY: Harper & Row.

Caplan, N.; Whitmore, J.; Bui, Q.; and Trautmann, M. (1985) "Scholastic Achievement Among the Children of Southeast Asian Refugees." Ann Arbor: Institute for Social Research.

Chavkin, N.F., and Williams, D.L., Jr. (1989) "Essential Elements of Strong Parent Involvement Programs," *Educational Leadership*, October, pp. 18-20.

Chavkin, N.F., and Williams, D.L., Jr. (1988) "Critical Issues in Teacher Training for Parent Involvement," *Educational Horizons*, vol. 66, pp. 87-89.

Chavkin, N.F., and Williams, D.L., Jr. "Low-Income Parents' Attitudes toward Parent Involvement in Education," *Journal of Sociology & Social Welfare*, 17-28.

Clapp, B. (1989) "The Discipline Challenge." *Instructor*, vol. XCIX (2), pp. 32-34.

Coleman, James and others. (1966) *Equality of Educational Opportunity*. Washington, D.C.: Office of Education.

Collins, C.H., Moles, O.C., and Cross, M. (1982) *The Home-School Connection: Selected Partnership Programs in Large Cities*. Boston, MA: Institute for Responsive Education.

Education Week (1985) "Changing Course, A 50-State Survey of Reform Measures." February 6, pp. 11-29.

Epstein, J. (1983) *Effects on Parents of Teacher Practices in Parent Involvement*. Center for Social Organization of Schools. Baltimore, MD: Johns Hopkins University.

Gallup, A. (1989) "The Second Gallup/Phi Delta Kappa Survey of Public School Teacher Opinion." *Phi Delta Kappan*, 79 (No. 11).

Goodlad, J.I. (1982) "An Agenda for Improving Our Schools." *Executive Review 2*, May.

Hanson, S.L., and Ginsburg, A. (1985) "Gaining Ground: Values and High School Success." Washington, D.C.: U.S. Department of Education.

Harris, L. ed., (1987) *The Metropolitan Life Survey of the American Teacher: Strengthening Lines Between Home and School*, New York: Metropolitan Life Insurance Company.

Henderson, A. (1987). *The Evidence Continues to Grow.* Columbia, MD: National Committee for Citizens in Education.

Herman, J., and Yeh, J., (1980) "Some Effects of Parent Involvement in Schools," Center for the Study of Evaluation, Graduate School of Education, University of California at Los Angeles, (ED 206 963).

Hewison, J. and Tizard, J. (1980) "Parental Involvement and Reading Attainment," *British Journal of Educational Psychology,* 50, 209-215.

Hispanic Policy Development Project (1990). *Together Is Better.* New York: NY.

Institute for Responsive Education (1982). *The Home-School Connection.* Boston: MA.

Institute for Responsive Education (1990). *Equity and Choice.* Vol. VI, Number 3. Boston: MA.

Kagan, S.L. *Parent Involvement Research: A Field In Search Of Itself.* Boston, MA: Institute for Responsive Education.

Krasnow, J. (1990) *Building Parent-Teacher Partnerships, Prospects for the Perspective of the Schools Reaching Out Project,* Boston, MA: Institute for Responsive Education.

Lombana, J.H. (1983) *Home-School Partnerships, Guidelines and Strategies for the Educator.* New York, NY: Grune & Stratton, Inc.

McAllister Swap, S. (1990) *Parent Involvement and Success for All Children, What We Know Now.* Boston, MA: Institute for Responsive Education.

McLaughlin, M. and Shields, P., (1987) "Involving Low-Income Parents in the Schools: A Role for Policy?," *Phi Delta Kappan,* October, pp. 156-160.

McLoughlin, C.S., Ph.D. (1987) *Parent-Teacher Conferencing.* Springfield, IL: Charles C. Thomas.

National Education Association (1983) "Nationwide Teacher Opinion Poll." Washington, D.C.

National School Boards Association (1988) *First Teachers: Parental Involvement In The Public Schools.* Alexandria: VA.

Rich, D. (1988) *MegaSkills: How Families Can Help Children Succeed in School and Beyond.* Boston, MA: Houghton Mifflin Company.

Rich, D. (1987) *Teachers and Parents: An Adult-to-Adult Approach.* National Education Association of the United States. The Home and School Institute.

Sanford Dornbusch et al., (1987) "The Relation of Parenting Style to Adolescent School Performance," *Child Development,* vol. 58, pp. 1244-57.

Seeley, D.S. (1985) *Education Through Partnership.* Washington, DC: American Enterprise Institute for Public Policy Research.

Smith, M.B. (1968) "School and Home: Focus on Achievement." *Developing Programs for the Educationally Disadvantaged.* New York, NY: Teachers College Press.

Thomas, W.B. (1980) "Parental and Community Involvement: Rx for Better School Discipline," *Phi Delta Kappan,* November, 203-204.

United States Department of Education (1986) *What Works: Research About Teaching and Learning.* Washington, D.C.

Walberg, H. (1984) "Improving the Productivity of America's Schools." *Educational Leadership* 41.

Welch, F.C., Ph.D. and Tisdale, P.C., Ph.D. (1986) *Between Parent and Teacher.* Springfield, IL: Charles C. Thomas.

Index

Parents On Your Side